PASTRY JIGGERS
AND PASTRY PRINTS

Pastry Jiggers and Pastry Prints

*THE EDITION IS LIMITED
TO 500 COPIES*

of which this is

No 98.

Michael Finlay

PASTRY JIGGERS
AND PASTRY PRINTS

MICHAEL FINLAY

PLAINS BOOKS
www.michaelfinlay.com
Contact: jmichaelfinlay@aol.com

Pastry Jiggers and Pastry Prints

First published 2014.

© Michael Finlay.

British Library Cataloguing in Publication Data
A catalogue record for this book is available
from the British Library.

ISBN-13: 978 1 872477 03 9

All rights reserved. No part of this publication may be reproduced in any form or by any means, without the prior permission of the author.

All photographs, other than those otherwise credited, are by the author.

Designed and computer-typeset by the author using Microsoft Publisher 2010 software.

Printed by H. & H. Reeds Printers Ltd., Penrith, Cumbria and bound by Charles Letts & Co. Ltd., Dalkieth.

CONTENTS

Acknowledgements	viii
Introduction	1
Plates - Metal and wood jiggers	6
Recipes using jiggers	56
Author's collection - pastry samples	67
Plates - Scrimshaw jiggers	75
Bibliography	79
Index	81

ACKNOWLEDGEMENTS

Alice Bleuzen, Silver Department, Sotheby's, Bill Brown, Bob Brown, Robin Butler, Roderick Butler, Vin Calcutt, Peter Cameron, Peter Campbell, Phil Chaney, Professor Rachel Cowgill of the University of Huddersfield, Tony Cowdry, Giles Cowley, Andrew J. Crawforth, always willing to share his extensive knowledge, Carl J. Davis, Ivan Day of Historic Food, for much help and encouragement, Robert Deeley, Bev Dennison, Alistair Dickenson, Don Fielding, Brian Ferguson, Abigail Fernández Fitó of George East Housewares, Ltd., Julia Gant, Anna Lloyd-Griffiths of the Fitzwilliam Museum, Cambridge, Andrew Grainger, Phillipa Grimstone of the Pepys Library, Cambridge, Gary Hahn, Keith Hockin, Julia Hoffbrand and Julia Hoffmeister of the Museum of London, Carole Holt of Carole's Country Store, Wilmington, Delaware, Terry and Marie Kelly, Stefan Koller of Koller Auctions, Zurich, Gary Loftus of Andrew Smith & Son, Auctioneers, Winchester, Philip Marshall, Maurice R. Meslans, Peter Nelson, Paul L. Moore, Sarah Orton of Gloucester City and Folk Museum, Helen Parkin of the British Museum, Angus Patterson of the V. & A. Museum, London, David Pearsall, Dr. M. Faye Prior of the York Castle Museum, Mark Procknik of the New Bedford Whaling Museum, Renato Rabiotti, for his unstinting help and enthusiasm, Dale Robson, John Rogers, Jan Rüttinger of the Museum der Brotkultur, Ulm, Dr. Katherine Schofield of King's College, London, Chris Scott and John Stephen, Crathes Castle, Eve Stone Antiques, East Haven, Connecticut, Steve Summerson-Wright, Christopher Sykes, D. F. Wallis, Dave Westle, Wynyard R.T. Wilkinson, Sue and Mike Witt, Andrew Wojtunik of the New Bedford Whaling Museum, and finally to my long-suffering wife Ann, who once more has risen to the task of proof-reading and has made many helpful suggestions.

INTRODUCTION

> **THOMAS BINGHAM,**
> Son and Succeffor to Mr. ABEL BINGHAM, deceafed;
> **IRONMONGER, BRASIER, and TOYMAN,**
> In MIDDLE-ROW, HOLBORN, LONDON:
>
> MAKES and fells all Sorts of fine Steel Chains and Keys for Watches; fine Steel and Brafs Stove Grates of all Sorts; Foreft Hearths for Wood or Scotch Coal, of the neweft Fafhion; Fire Shovels, Tongs and Pokers; Neat pierce Work in Steel or Brafs, and Wire Fenders; Fine wrought Brafs Arms, Brafs Curtain-rings, Brafs and japan'd Hooks for Chimneys, Hats, Pictures, of all Sorts; Kitchen Furniture of all Sorts, viz. Ranges, Cranes, Smoak-jacks, and others; Racks, Spits, Coppers, Boilers, Stewing Stoves, Fifh Kettles, and Carp-pans; French and other Stew-pans, Frying-pans, Sauce-pans, Preferving-pans, Copper and Iron Dripping-pans, Copper Drinking-pots, Coffee and Chocolate-pots, Coffee-mills, Fritter and Pudding-moulds, Turnip fcoops, Bread-rafps and Graters; Apple-coarers, Jagging-irons, Pafte-prints, Lemon-racers, Doubing Larding-pins, Toafting-irons, Flefh-forks, Steak-tongs, Cuckolds and Pins; Grooved and other Grid-irons, Pig-plates, Salamanders, Tea-kettles, Trivets, Box-irons and Flat-irons; Cafe Knives and Forks of all Sorts; Brafs Ladles and Baifters, Skimmers, Slices, Pepper and Drudgers, Candle-boxes, Warming-pans, Peftles and Mortars, Brafs Cocks, Iron Skewers, Cleavers, Chopping-knives, Vent Pegs and Ventilators, Scales and Weights: A very great Variety of curious Japans in Waiters, Kettles, and Lamps, Urns, Tea Kitchens, Coffee-pots, Bread-bafkets, Candlefticks, Dreffing-boxes, Tea-chefts, Ink-ftands, Snuff Boxes, Salts, Bottle-tickets, &c. by the moft eminent Hands: Fine Steel and Brafs Candlefticks of all Sorts; Screw Spring Snuffers and Stands: Variety of Salvers, Tea-kettles, Lamps, Coffee-pots, Tankards, Candle-fticks, Sauce-boats, Caftors, &c. in French Plate, not to be difcerned from real Silver, and Variety of Stew-pans, Sauce-pans, Candlefticks, &c. plated with folid Silver: Fine chafed and wrought brown Tea-kettles, Lamps, Urns, Tea-kitchens, Coffee-pots, Tea Equipages well coloured and of the neweft Fafhion: Copper, Iron, and japaned Coal Scoops, Plate Warmers, Camp Chaffing-difhes, Shade and Machine Candlefticks, Sugar Hatchets, Key-fwivels, Corkfcrews, Wine-Coopers-knippers, fine fteel plated Metal, Silver and Stone Buckles of the neweft Fafhion: work'd Gold and Silver Sleeve Buttons, Ear-rings and Necklaces, and Variety of Jewellers Work; Piftols and Pocket Tinder-boxes, Steel Pencil-cafes, and Black Lead Pen-cils, Razors, Pen-knives, Sciffors and Nut-crackers, Hones and Straps, Brafs and Leather Dog-collars, Curling and Pinching Irons, Powder-flafks and Shot-pouches, neat Steel Collars for young Ladies, Cruet-ftands of all Sorts: Ivory Pocket-books, Pocket-glaffes, Spectacles, Smelling-bottles, Toothpick-cafes, Spanifh and Morocco Books, with or without Inftruments. Bells hung in the neateft and beft Manner, and Tinning in general.

1 Trade card of Thomas Bingham, Ironmonger, Brasier and Toyman, London, 18th century. Among his wide-ranging stock-in-trade are "Jagging-irons" and "Paste-prints".
© *The Trustees of the British Museum*

TERMINOLOGY

The use of pastry jiggers goes back to at least the 16th Century and they have been known by many different names. Bartolomeo Scappi, chef to Pope Pius V, in his *Opera* of 1570, captions his illustration of one as *"Sperone da pasticiero"* or the pastrycook's spur. (p. 8) The jigger's wheel can certainly be reminiscent of the rowel of a spur. Another, he calls simply a *"Sperone da pasta"*, a pastry spur.

2 Three views of a late 18th-/early 19th-century treen apple or vegetable peeler cut from a mahogany-like tropical hardwood, with sheet-iron cutter. It is inlaid with a pewter anchor and this and the presence of hearts as decoration indicate that it was probably made by a sailor as a love token for his wife or girl probably while away at sea, and the abalone shell mother-of pearl inlays suggest that he may have been a long way from home. As a kitchen device, the spur-like decoration can only be his interpretation of a pastry jigger. It may perhaps be somewhat fanciful to see the chip-carved decoration as a rudimentary navette or boat form beside a large finned creature, presumably a whale? 266mm.

Author's Collection.

The pointed rowel of a horseman's spur in the late 16th century might be difficult to see as a useful pastry wheel, but such pastry tools were made. A fine 17th-century Dutch example with its finial in the form of a contemporary pastry chef, leaves no doubt as to its function. (p. 15) In modern times some equestrian spurs are marketed as having "Pastry-wheel" rowels. It would appear that the pastry wheel has come full circle, so to speak.

What we would now refer to as a crimper, with a tweezer-like nipping action, Scappi calls a *"Molete per pasta"*, about which more later.

NOMENCLATURE

Until relatively recently the commonly-used word for what is now more usually referred to as "pastry" was simply "paste". Hence we have paste jiggers, and in the U.S.A., paste jaggers, names used in trade catalogues until about the end of the 19th Century, now more commonly referred to as pastry jiggers or pastry jaggers. Other terms occasionally found are: coggling wheels, dough wheels, dough cutters, dough spurs, gigling irons, jagging irons, jagging wheels, pie crimpers, pie sealers and pie trimmers. It should be noted that in spite of the use of "irons" to describe them, the vast majority of the pastry jiggers which turn up today are mainly made of some form of copper alloy, iron or steel examples being relatively uncommon.

The term "jagger", no doubt derived from the jagged edge produced by its use, is perhaps more appropriate than the commonly-used "jigger", as has been pointed out in the past. In the late 19th-century Encyclopædia of Practical Cookery, exactly this observation is made.

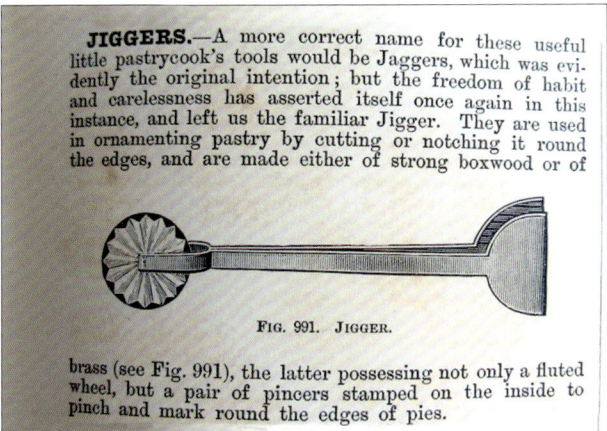

3 From the *Encyclopædia of Practical Cookery,* edited by Theodore Francis Garrett, published in London in 1892.

Courtesy Ivan Day Collection

The second revised edition of Dr. Samuel Johnson's Dictionary of the English Language, edited by Henry John Todd in 1827, makes no mention of a pastry jagging iron, but defines the verb "To jagg" (which he derives from the Welsh *gagau,* slits or holes) as "to cut into indentures; to cut into teeth like those of a saw", citing Sir Francis Bacon. A year later, however, in his The Dialect of Craven, in the West Riding of Yorkshire, by "A native of Craven", actually William Carr, M.A., of Bolton Abbey, "Jagging iron" is defined as "A circular instrument with teeth used in forming ornamental pastry", with a reference to the Todd derivation above.

The term "jigger", however, still seems to be the term universally used, at least in the UK, and is therefore the term generally used throughout this book.

USAGE

Each jigger has usually a number of elements, each of which has a different function:

The wheel

a   b   c

4 A variety of wheel design, single, double and ornamental.

Author's collection

Most jiggers have a wheel whose edge is a continuous design of 'Vs', which is used to cut through rolled-out pastry, leaving a jagged edge, from which the terms jagger and jigger are no doubt derived. (**4a**) Some jiggers have two wheels set side-by-side which enable strips of pastry with decorative edges, for use as lattice work on tarts, for example, to be cut with a single roll of the device. (**4b**) Those wheels with a more complex arrangement of 'Vs', often in groups of three, tend to be earlier. (**4c**)

It has often been written that the wheel may also be used to roll round the edge of a pie to seal it or to impress designs on its crust. Anyone who tries to use the wheel in this way will find that it is almost impossible to avoid cutting entirely through the pastry. In the late 19th century, the addition of a fluted drum centred on the wheel did allow a pie crust to be trimmed, crimped and sealed with one action. Many patents based on this design appeared, mainly in America. (page 50)

The function of the wheel is intended purely as a cutting instrument, although a segment of the wheel may be used flatly to impress a radiating fan design.

The print

5 Four various matrices of pastry prints, three from cruciform jiggers, the square one from an individual stamp.

Author's collection

The "Paste-prints" offered for sale by Thomas Bingham in his trade card (Plate **1**) are most probably those devices, often without wheels, which have a stamp of circular, square or lozenge form, often with a chequered design, with which to impress the pastry. Some jiggers, often of cruciform design and substantial size, are also fitted with "prints". (See pages 33 to 37)   The prints can be used singly or together to create a variety of patterns.

Arced, straight and angled cutters

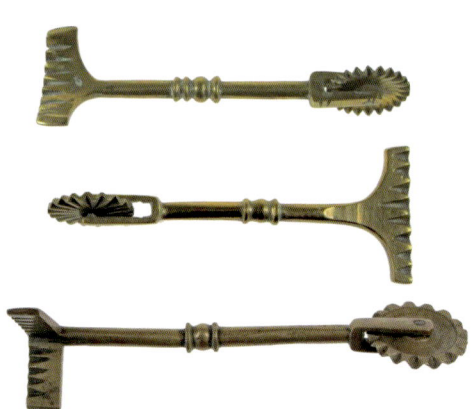

6 Three jiggers with simple forms of cutter, arced, straight or angled.

Author's collection

Many of the traditional small brass jiggers have a wheel at one end and a fixed cutter with a similar continuous 'Vs' cutting edge, usually of arced form but occasionally straight or angled, which can also, when applied vertically, be used to cut out shapes to be applied to the crust of a pie. They may also be applied horizontally to the edge of a pie crust to create a decorative edge and to seal the pie firmly at the same time.

Shape cutters and markers

7 A selection of the many varieties of shape cutters available in the late 19th century.

Author's collection

Some jiggers have a wheel at one end and a shape cutter at the other, which may be geometrical in design or more organic, as leaf forms for example. In the late 19th century these were marketed as part of complete jiggers or separately with sockets for attachment to jiggers. (See p. 28) Similar cutters were available without any means of attachment, as "Fancy markers" but with relatively sharp edges which tend to cut right through the pastry rather than merely impress the design.

Somewhat less commonly found are markers which are clearly intended merely to impress the pastry rather than cut out the overall shape.

Crimpers

8 A late 18th- or early 19th-century jigger with a simple crimper, in this case in iron, much less common than similar brass jiggers.

Author's collection

Those jiggers combining a cutting wheel at one end and tweezer-like crimpers at the other are among the most common types of jigger. Crimpers have a long history. Scappi, in his *Opera* of 1570, illustrates one without a wheel which he calls a *"Molete per pasta"*. (See p. 10) Later examples of such crimpers can be found and used to create a decorative edge on a single layer of pastry or to seal the joining of two layers where both layers are accessible, as in the case of a pasty for example.

The remnants of what was patently a much larger

9 Two views of a group of 19th-/20th-century brass crimpers, numbered "11" to "15" and patently part of a much larger set.

MF 221-225

set, dating from perhaps the late 19th or early 20th century, have shaped grips to create a variety of effects. These could be used on either pastry or fondant decoration of cakes, by inserting the tips of the crimper, slightly open, into the pastry or fondant and gently squeezing, a series of such producing a raised ornamentation.

Jiggers as dough knives

Some jiggers are designed to cut dough into workable portions, with a sickle-like blade. This is one of the earliest designs, also illustrated by Scappi. (See page 8)

DATING

Pastry jiggers in the form of a cutting wheel on a handle have a long history and dating of particular specimens is often difficult. Once the design had developed into an efficient form, there would be no need to make significant changes over a long period of time. Trade catalogues are helpful in giving illustrations of those implements available at a particular time, but expensively produced engravings were often re-used over considerable periods. Auction catalogues often describe as Georgian, jiggers which may still be found in late 19th-century trade catalogues, and in some cases, this may be a reasonable description.

In the present work, the author has given his best estimates of the probable date range of the jiggers illustrated, based on what evidence is available, and with the experience of a lifetime of collecting and handling antique metalwork. Nonetheless, dating should be regarded as having a degree of latitude.

PLATES
Metal and wooden jiggers

10 Engraved plate from Bartolomeo Scappi's *Opera* of 1570 showing a pastrycook's table with pastry jigger and crimper and another with a tart made with the jigger.

Courtesy Google Books

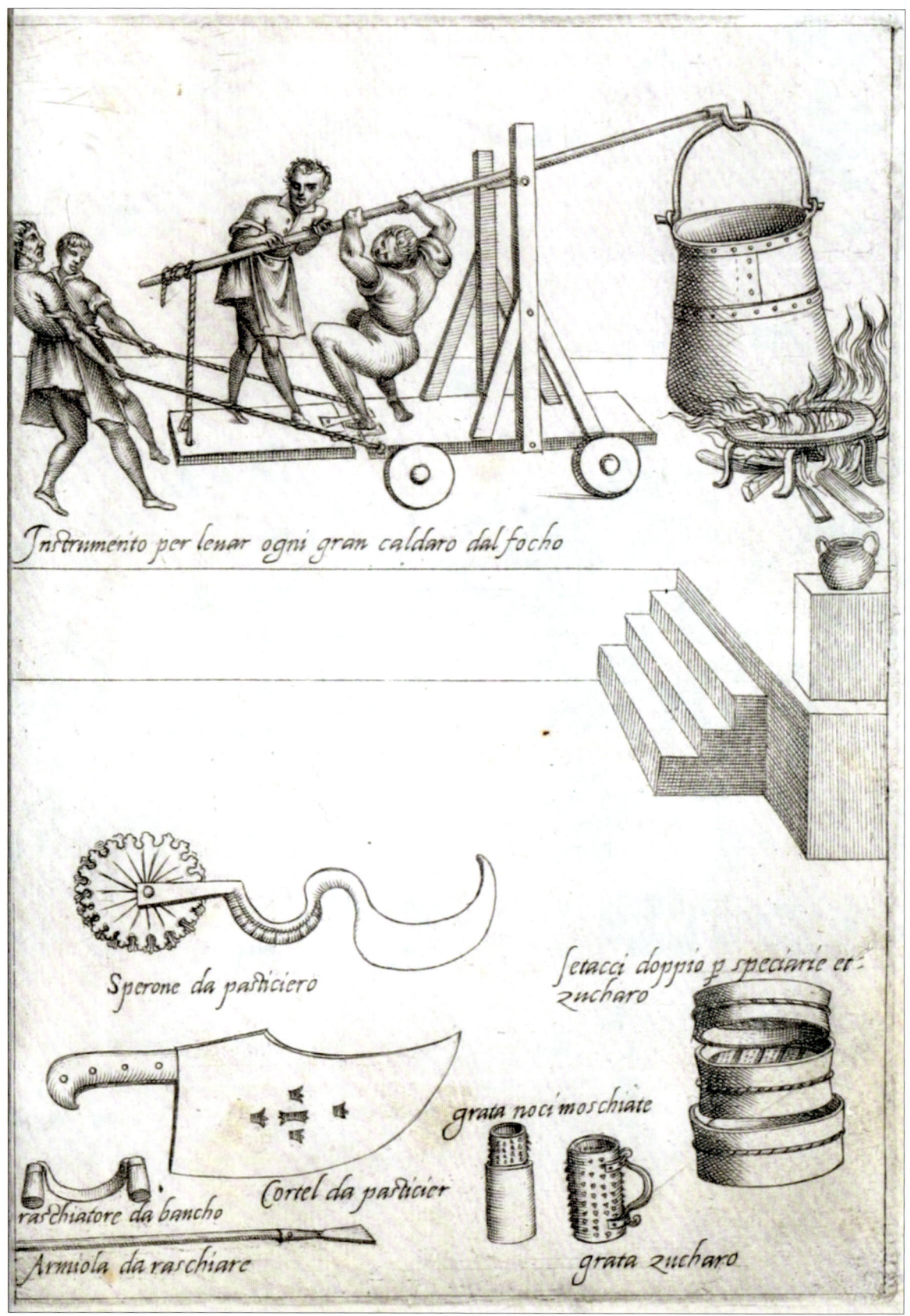

11 Plate from Scappi's *Opera* of 1570 showing a jigger called *Sperone da pasticiero,* literally "spur of the pastrycook", and a pastry knife.

Courtesy Google Books

Pastry Jiggers and Pastry Prints

In general shape all of the zoomorphic jiggers on this page are very similar to that of Benvenuto Scappi's example opposite, described as *"Sperone da pasticiero"*, with ornate cutting wheel and sickle-like terminal for trimming surplus pastry from the edge of a dish as well as for cutting straight edges and dividing dough. The word *"sperone"* is also used for the rowel of a riding spur, a connection not difficult to see. The type was still being made in simpler form in the 18th century.

These jiggers, known as *"Coqs"*, based on a stylised cockerel form, are first found in Italy and were adopted in France, from whence the name *"Coq de pâtissier"* derives.

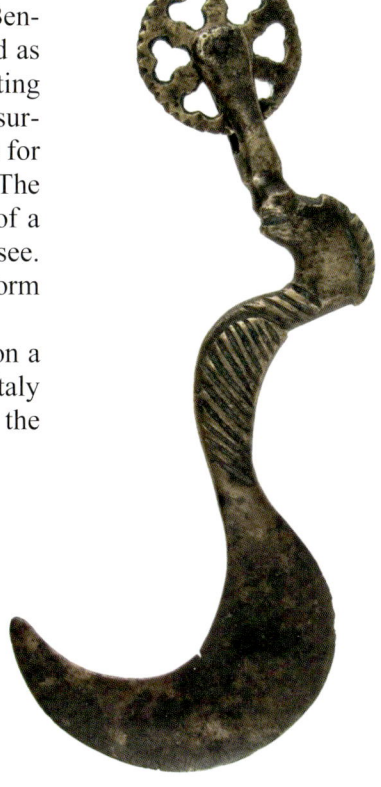

12 A rare Italian pastry jigger or *Sperone da Pasticiero*, of *Coq* form, late 16th Century. 137mm.
© *Trustees of the British Museum, Ref: 1877, 0802.14.*
⇦

13 An Italian bronze jigger of *Coq* form, late 16th century. 142mm
MF 230

14 A rare Italian bronze jigger of stylised *Coq* form, 16th century. 148mm.
MF 015
⇦

15 A rare Italian bronze jigger of *Coq* design, circa 1590. 125mm.
Courtesy Renato Rabaiotti

Note the similarity of the wheel to that of Plate **22**.

16 A rare Italian gilt-bronze jigger (now lacking wheel), the *Coq* devoured by a sea creature, engraved "S.L.O.P.", c. 1590. 102mm.
© *Courtesy the Trustees of the V. & A. Museum, Ref: M. 205-1927*

17 A French brass *Coq*, 18th Century. 108mm.
MF 180

9

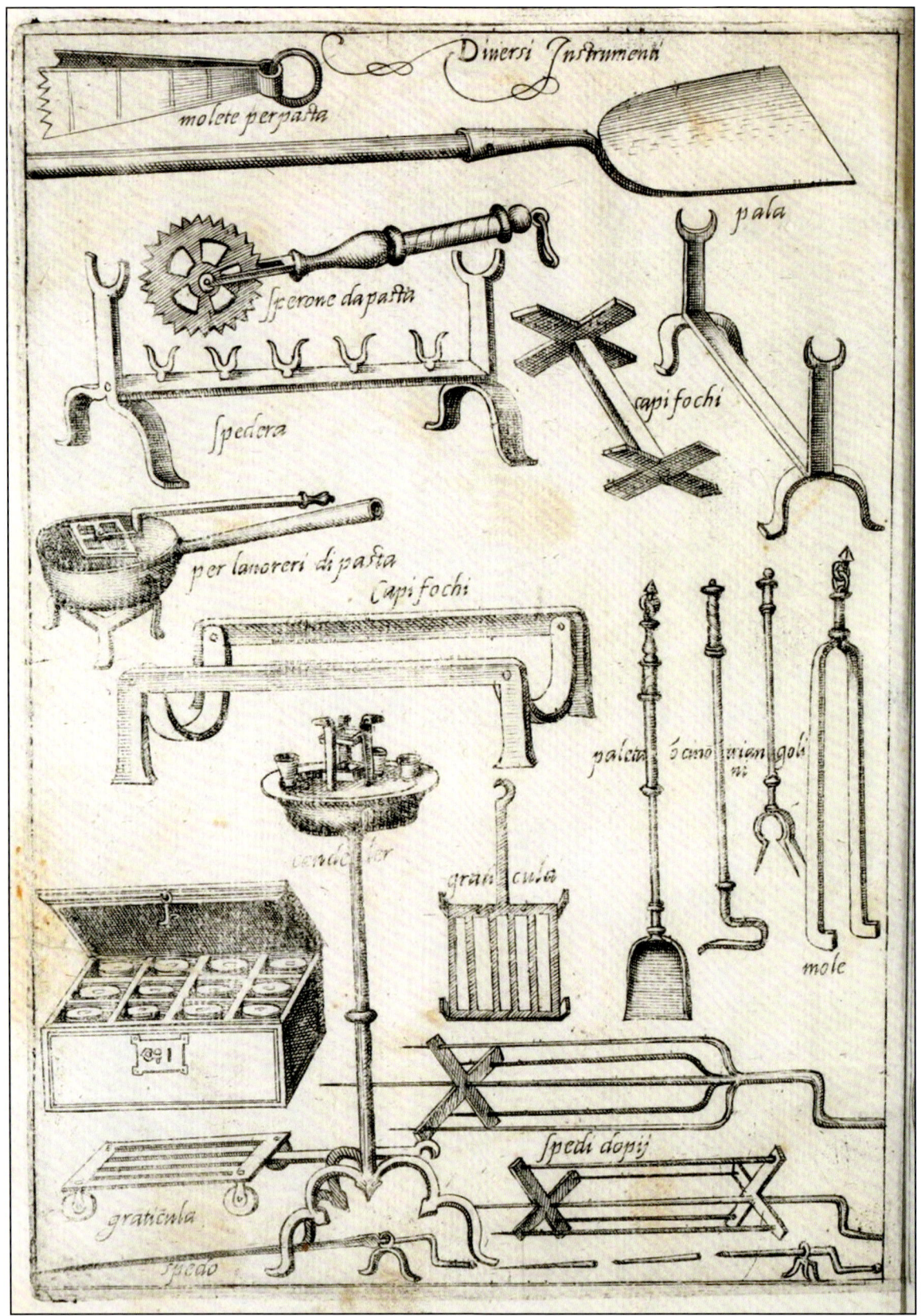

18 Plate from Scappi's *Opera* showing the *Molete per pasta* or crimper and another form of *Sperone da pasta* or jigger. Modern versions of both implements are still being used.

Courtesy Google Books

Pastry Jiggers and Pastry Prints

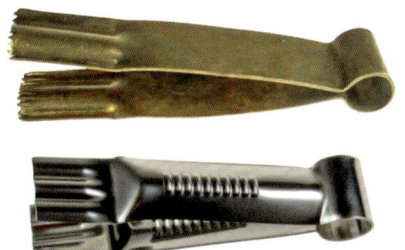

19 a & b A brass crimper similar in design to Scappi's *molete per pasta* of 1570, 19th century, 104mm, and a modern (2013) stainless steel example. 88mm.
They say there's nothing new under the sun.

MF 206 and 149

20 A late 17th-century brass jigger with ornately-cut wheel pattern, its balustroid handle not dissimilar to that of Scappi's illustration of 1570, opposite. 143mm.
© Trustees of the V. and A. Museum, Croft-Lyons Bequest, M 1034-1926

21 A 17th-century brass jigger with double balustroid handle. 120mm.
MF 135

22 a and b Two views of a very rare Italian (Sicilian) late 16th-/early 17th-century bronze jigger with figural stem and single cutting wheel. The small "print" at the base is of rosette design. 155mm.
© Trustees of the British Museum, Ref: 1878, 0903.29

The wheel form of the above example, of Moorish arcaded design, is also to be found on a jigger of *Coq* design of circa 1590. (see Plate **15,** page 9)

Jiggers of this type without figures but with multi-knopped stems and wheel supports of similar design are also known.

23 A very rare Italian late 16th-/early 17th-century bronze jigger with figural stem and two cutting wheels, for cutting strips of pastry. The small "print" at the base is of rosette design. 180mm.
Ex Nessi Collection, sold by Koller Auctions, Zurich, 2nd April, 2012, Lot 796.
MF 033

Pastry Jiggers and Pastry Prints

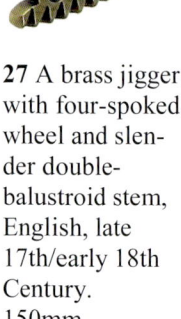

24 A rare cast-iron jigger from a turned pattern, the lower terminal in the form of a rosette stamp or print, Italian, 17th Century. 152mm.
MF 080

25 A brass jigger of octagonally-faceted form with chequered print, probably Italian, 17th Century. 118mm.
MF 083

26 Brass jigger with cast convoluted wheel and slender balustroid stem, 17th Century. 135mm.
MF 105

27 A brass jigger with four-spoked wheel and slender double-balustroid stem, English, late 17th/early 18th Century. 150mm.
MF 007

28 A 17th-century copper-alloy jigger with double balustroid stem, the wheel with unusually convoluted design, an early feature, as may be seen in Scappi's illustration of his "Sperone da pasticiero". 123mm.
MF 081

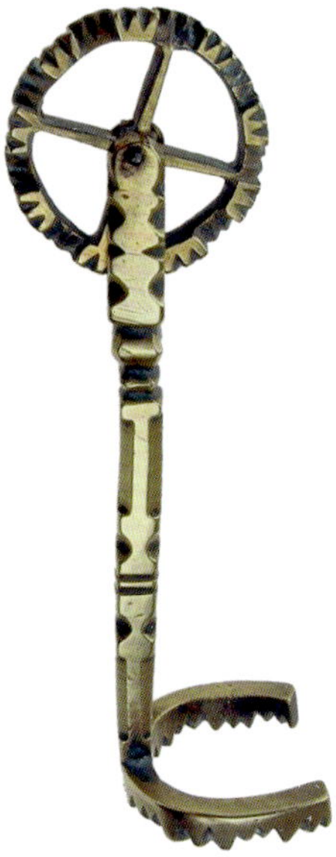

29 A brass jigger with convoluted four-spoked wheel, faceted stem, and horseshoe shaped print, Scandinavian, late 17th Century. 115mm.
MF 001

30 The lower section of a similar jigger to that shown right, in excavated condition. Note that both jiggers have nicks filed into the edges, at approximately two thirds of the crimper height, the use of which is not apparent. They may have been simply to allow uniform alignment with the edge of the pastry when crimping the edge. 64mm.
MF 112

31 A brass jigger with finely-faceted stem and elongated crimper of shovel form, 17th Century. 142mm.
MF 111

32 Part only of a brass jigger with four-spoked wheel, Scandinavian, late 17th Century. 90mm.
MF 110

33 A brass jigger with finely faceted stem, late 17th/early 18th century. 134mm.
MF 034

Pastry Jiggers and Pastry Prints

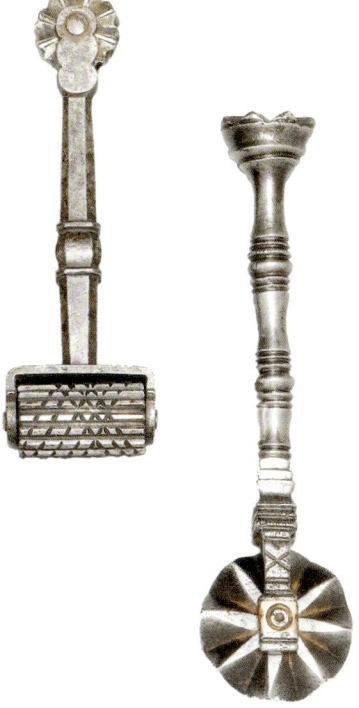

34 A part brass jigger found in a Dutch house wall built in 1702. 17th century. 72mm.
Courtesy Ivan Day Collection

35 a and b Two rare wrought-iron jiggers, from the Nessi Collection, that on the right with bronze inlays, French or Spanish, 18th century. 115mm & 140mm.
Sold 2nd April, 2012, Lot 795, for 800 Swiss Francs.
Courtesy Koller Auctions, Zurich

36 A copper-alloy jigger with two wheels and facet-cut stem, late 17th Century. 140mm.
MF 117

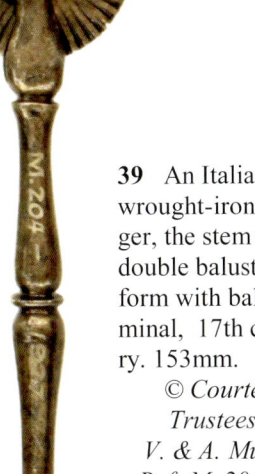

37 and detail A rare Italian iron jigger with broad decorative wheel, with tang for a wooden handle, now lacking, 17th century. 171mm.
© *Courtesy the Trustees of the V. & A. Museum, Ref: M. 203-1927*

38 A rare Italian wrought-iron pastry cutter in the form of an entwined snake holding a fan-shaped cutter / crimper in its mouth, inscribed "ALLERIA", 17th century. 125mm.
© *Courtesy the Trustees of the V. and A. Museum. Ref: 105-1884*

39 An Italian wrought-iron jigger, the stem of double balustroid form with ball terminal, 17th century. 153mm.
© *Courtesy the Trustees of the V. & A. Museum, Ref: M. 204-1927*

40 A fine and rare combination pastry jigger and herb chopper with bronze wheel and handle, the steel blade also usable as a dough knife, French, circa 1710. 195mm high.
Courtesy Renato Rabaiotti

13

41 Engraving from La Varenne's *Le Pâtissier François,* published in Paris in 1653 and again by the Elzevier Press in Amsterdam in 1655. Note the use of a spiked jigger.
Courtesy the Bibliotèque Nationale, Paris

Pastry Jiggers and Pastry Prints

42 The *Officers of the Coopers' and Winecrackers' Guild, Amsterdam*, circa 1660, by Gerbrand van den Eeckhout, (1621-1674).

© *The National Gallery, London*

43 and detail A rare, possibly unique, Dutch figural brass jigger, its finial a half-length portrait of an artisan pastrycook with his rolling pin and folded pastry, with double-balustroid shank and heavy spiked wheel, mid 17th century. 140mm.

MF 030

Note the similarity of the costume of the guild officers in Gerbrand van den Eeckhout's group portrait (above) and that of the pastrycook of the jigger (left), both of the mid 17th century. The simple Puritan-style collar with double tassel between and the large wide-brimmed hats are very similar. The pastrycook's goatee beard is also typical of the period.

A spiked wheel as opposed to a wavy-edged one is not common, but seems to have been fashionable at this time; a similar device is to be seen in the engraving of *Le Pâtissier François* of 1655, (opposite). The double-balustroid stem is also a 17th-century form.

Pastry Jiggers and Pastry Prints

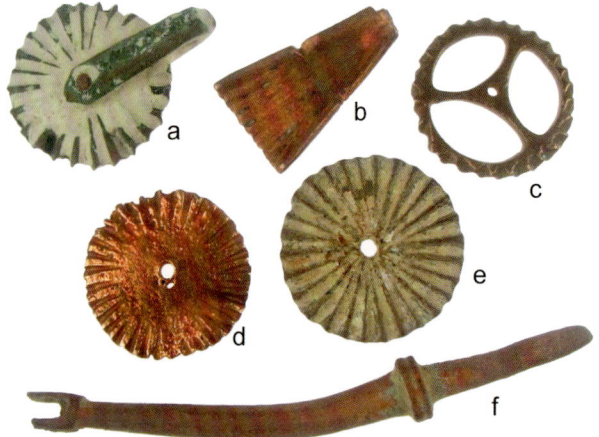

44 A group of copper-alloy metal-detecting finds:
a, c, d and e. Four wheels from pastry jiggers, all excavated in England.
b is a cutter/crimper from a late 17th-century pastry jigger of similar type to those of Plates **30** and **31**.
f is the stem, part of the wheel supports and handle tang of a wheeled device, most probably a pastry jigger. It would have had a turned wooden handle which would have rotted away during burial.

It is not at all uncommon for parts of pastry jiggers to turn up at metal-detecting rallies and among individual detecting enthusiasts. It is unlikely that anyone would have been using a jigger *al fresco* and one may only speculate as to the reason for their relative commonness as detecting finds. The most likely explanation is that they are probably the surviving parts of jiggers accidentally discarded with kitchen waste, vegetable peelings and the like. They would then find their way on to the household midden, and eventually be scattered with its composted contents on to the field to be broken up by the action of the plough and harrow.

The author has heard other theories, including the possibility of jiggers being accidentally lost during the clearance of villages to create sophisticated landscaping of stately homes, but this would not account for the wide distribution of such finds, nor for the relatively large numbers involved.

The extensive presence of such finds may be a somewhat strange phenomenon, but it does not surprise the present author. Out of a dozen teaspoons which formed part of a canteen of flatware, received as a wedding present over half a century ago, only a couple remain, and it is entirely possible that the rest were inadvertently thrown out with kitchen waste.

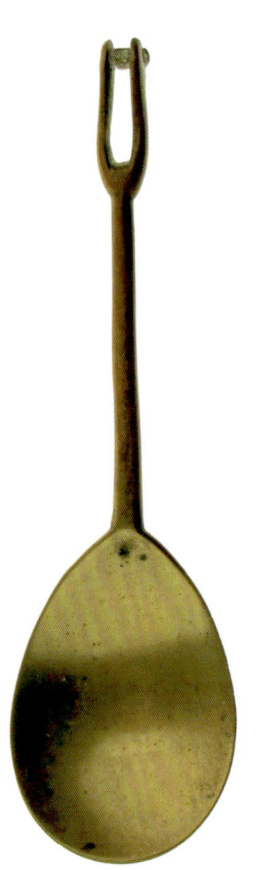

45 A latten spoon, lacking its former pastry wheel, 17th century. 133mm. Note the lack of stem decoration.

Courtesy Roderick Butler

46 A combination latten jigger and spoon, late 17th Century, of identical design to that of Plate **45**, the wheel with slightly larger dentation. 150mm.

Courtesy the Fitzwilliam Museum, Cambridge, A.F. de Navarro Bequest, Ref: NAV. S.30-1933

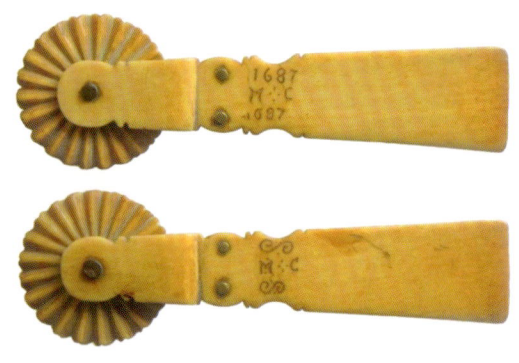

47 Two views of a unique Charles II ivory pastry wheel with ownership initials and and dated 1687, the handle of finely-serrated crimper form.

Courtesy Edward Harrison Collection

16

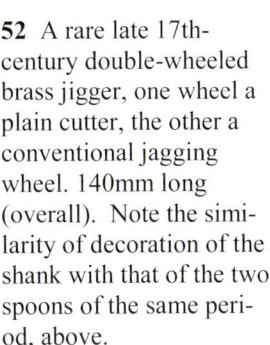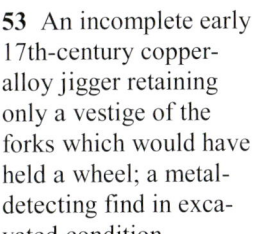

48 A combination latten jigger and spoon, late 17th century. Note the extensive wear of the axis hole, typical of many early jiggers. 150mm.

MF 054

49 A combination latten jigger and spoon, late 17th century. 150mm.

MF 188

50 A mid 17th-century latten combined spoon and pastry jigger in excavated condition, the spoon with typical fig-shaped bowl and double-balustroid stem. It is a metal-detecting find from the Thames foreshore near London Bridge. 175mm.

MF 023

51 A brass jigger formerly with two wheels, with double balustroid stem, initialled RB and indistinctly dated 167?. 147mm.

Courtesy Roderick Butler

52 A rare late 17th-century double-wheeled brass jigger, one wheel a plain cutter, the other a conventional jagging wheel. 140mm long (overall). Note the similarity of decoration of the shank with that of the two spoons of the same period, above.

Courtesy Gloucester City Museums, Gloucester Folk Museum, Ref: F00033

53 An incomplete early 17th-century copper-alloy jigger retaining only a vestige of the forks which would have held a wheel; a metal-detecting find in excavated condition.

MF 190

Pastry Jiggers and Pastry Prints

55 a - d A group of four similar copper-alloy jiggers which may be dated to the late 17th century. Note the similarity of stem formation with that of the spoon (left), and the shapes of the stamps with that of the silver example of 1683, (below right). The bronze-like colour of these jiggers may indicate a bronze alloy but could be the result of leaching of copper to the surface as a result of burial. The third example is a metal-detecting find, as may be the others. Each about 125mm.

MF 022, 123, 091 and 130

54 A latten combined pastry jigger and spoon of the late 17th century. There is extensive wear to the axis hole of the wheel mount, a common feature of early jiggers. 148mm.   *MF 154*

56 a and b Two views of an extremely rare silver jigger with typical late 17th-century engraved stylised foliate decoration, hallmarked London, 1683, maker's mark AB in monogram. 120mm. Illustrated anonymously in *The Collector's Dictionary of the Silver and Gold of Great Britain and North America* by Michael Clayton, Country Life, 1971, p. 36, where the maker's mark was incorrectly given as AH.

Sold at Christies' South Kensington, 13th July, 2006, as part of the James Walker Collection, where the maker's mark was correctly given as AB conjoined, for £3,500 plus premium etc. It was next sold as part of the Stanley J. Seeger Collection (1000 Ways of Seeing), Sotheby's, London, 5th and 6th March, 2014, Lot 500, to the London trade, where the price realised was also £3,500.

Subsequently purchased by the author from Alastair Dickenson, Jermyn Street, London silver specialist.

MF 215

Other silver jiggers exist, of similar design to the Walker/Seeger example shown opposite, Plates **56 a** and **b),** but of less convincing proportions and lacking its period vigour. One example, with a maker's mark only, which has been tentatively ascribed to the silversmith Sarah Holaday and dated to circa 1720, is illustrated in *The Albert Collection—500 years of British and European Silver,* by Robin Butler, 2004, p. 143. The engraving of simple lines in place of the V-cuts which produce the jagged edge when cutting pastry, and the rudimentary wheel suggest a lack of understanding by its maker of its function, and one is forced to question whether or not it is a modern copy of the Walker example illustrated in Clayton's Dictionary

A third example, close in design to the Albert Collection jigger, also lacking the vigour of the Walker specimen, bearing hallmarks for London, 1766, maker's mark rubbed, was sold at Dukes Auctioneers, Dorchester, on 27th November, 2008, lot 186, for £360.

57 A silver jigger with maker's mark only, "MJ?", the stem faceted with shell-form print, late 17th-/early 18th century. 111mm.

MF 179

58 A fine silver jigger with heart-shaped cutter, with the unidentified maker's mark "SA", possibly American Colonial in origin, late 17th /early 18th century. 140mm. 1.32 ozs Troy

© *Maurice R. Meslans*

59 An unmarked silver jigger, engraved with ownership initials, "ED", late 17th century. 110mm.

MF 037

60 An unmarked silver jigger with octagonally-faceted stem, late 17th century. 120mm.

© *York Museums Trust (York Castle Museum) Ref: 1976/774*

By any standards, the pastry jigger would normally fall into the category of a fairly lowly piece of kitchen equipment and it is therefore not surprising that silver examples are very rare. One can only speculate who might have used them. A working silversmith might well have made one as a special present for his wife or girlfriend, and that above, with its heart-shaped cutter, may be such an example.

One can imagine that some of the elegant and presumably wealthy "Ladies and Gentlewomen Practitioners In the Art of Pastery and Cookery" attending Nathaniel Meystnor's cookery school in the late 17th century might well have aspired to a silver jigger; one lady depicted in his invitation (Plate **61**) certainly seems eager to display hers.

61 An engraved trade card in the form of an invitation to ladies, by Nathaniel Meystnor, to partake of the work of his scholars, the "Ladies and Gentlewomen Practitioners in the Art of Pastery and Cookery". The highly-ornamented pies and confections illustrated are typical of the period, circa 1680. The card was in the Samuel Pepys Collection and must therefore predate his death in 1703.

James Hakewill, in his *History of Windsor,* 1813, records that a Mr. Meystnor contributed £20 towards the building of a new Guildhall there in 1686.

© *The Pepys Library, Magdalene College, Cambridge*

62 A pie made by the author, with "haystack" pouring funnel for the final jelly, which also acts as an outlet for steam, the latter's rim cut with the jigger shown above.
Photograph, the author

63 A 19th-century brass jigger of simple form with large teeth, used by the author to cut the "haystack" rim, left. 180mm.
MF 064

61 (Detail) The lady student, in all her finery, centre-right in Meystnor's trade card, is holding a jigger, with what, at its lower end, one might at first glance suppose is a toothed cutter, having upward-facing teeth. On closer examination, however, it is clear that this is unaligned with, and detached from, the stem of the jigger.

A more appropriate explanation had been afforded by the food historian, Ivan Day. The object is in fact a type of pastry funnel, known at the time as a "haystack", with jigger-cut dentate rim, luted into a piercing in the top of the shaped pie, for the dual purposes of allowing steam to escape and of easing the pouring in of jelly.

A 17th-century depiction of such a pie with a haystack, in a still-life of kitchen utensils and produce, entitled *Bodegón con la Verdura,* by Antonio Pereda y Segado, (1611-1678), is in the Museo Nacionale de Arte Antiga, in Lisbon.

64 A woodcut of two pies with "haystacks", from Robert May's *The Accompisht Cook or the Art & Mystery of Cookery,* London, 1685.
Courtesy Ivan Day Collection

Pastry Jiggers and Pastry Prints

65 A brass jigger with ring-turned balustroid stem, c. 1800. 91mm.
MF 165

66 A brass jigger with ring-turned cylindrical stem, c. 1800. 103mm.
MF 184

67 A two-wheeled brass jigger with lacquered finish, late 19th century. 111mm.
MF 131

68 An elegant late 18th-century brass jigger. 123mm.
MF 024

69 A two-wheeled brass jigger, late 19th-century. 106mm.
MF 211

70 a and b Two jiggers probably from the same foundry, early 19th century, the double-wheeled one of brass, 156mm, the single-wheeled, most unusually, of bronze. 150mm.
MF 074, 008

71 a and b Two brass jiggers of the late 19th century, with angled cutters, that on the left with plain reel knop, 125mm, the other with similar but knurled knop. 128mm.
MF 170, 126

72 A brass jigger with arced cutter, mid 19th century. 99mm.
MF 186

73 A brass jigger with straight cutter, mid 19th century. 125mm.
MF 119

74 A brass jigger with arced cutter, mid 19th century. 123mm.
MF 141

75 A brass wheel and handle as sold separately, mid 19th century. 100mm.
MF 195

76 Another, with straight cutter mid to late 19th century. 100mm.
MF 173

Pastry Jiggers and Pastry Prints

77 A mid 19th-century brass jigger with straight cutter. 100mm.
MF 057

78 An early 19th-century brass jigger with straight cutter. 116mm.
MF 212

79 An early 20th-century brass jigger with straight cutter. 100mm.
MF 174

80 An early 19th-century brass jigger with arced cutter. 127mm.
MF 122

81 An early to mid 19th-century brass jigger with arced cutter. 106mm.
MF 214

82 An early to mid 19th-century brass jigger with arced cutter. 111mm.
MF 175

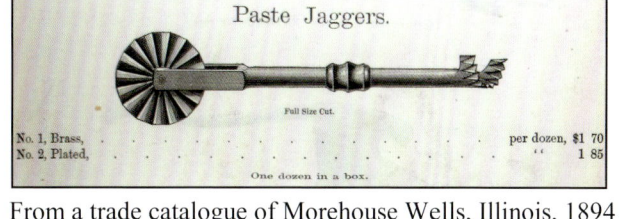

83 From a trade catalogue of Morehouse Wells, Illinois, 1894

84 An early 19th-century brass jigger with arced cutter. 113mm.
MF 176

85 A late 19th-century brass jigger with arced cutter. 98mm.
MF 071

86 A late 19th-century brass jigger with arced cutter. 100mm.
MF 177

87 A late 19th-century brass jigger with arced cutter. 100mm.
MF 020

88 A late 19th-century brass jigger with arced cutter. 104mm.
MF 178

Pastry Jiggers and Pastry Prints

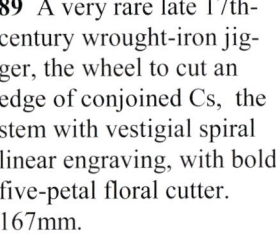

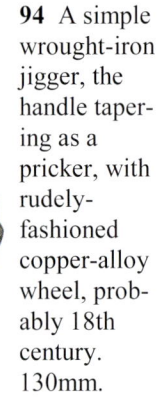

89 A very rare late 17th-century wrought-iron jigger, the wheel to cut an edge of conjoined Cs, the stem with vestigial spiral linear engraving, with bold five-petal floral cutter. 167mm.

MF 078

90 A very rare late 17th-/early 18th-century wrought-iron jigger with conventional wheel, also having spiral linear engraved decoration to the stem, the foot a tightly-curved arc to cut a horseshoe form. 150mm.

MF 082

91 - 93 Three rare 18th-century wrought-iron jiggers, of conventional forms more commonly found in brass. 122, 103 and 117mm.

MF 089, 088, and 090

94 A simple wrought-iron jigger, the handle tapering as a pricker, with rudely-fashioned copper-alloy wheel, probably 18th century. 130mm.

MF 192

It is probable that the two jiggers above are of French origin. An identical example to that on the right, probably the same one, is illustrated as part of his collection of *"Roulettes de pâtissier"* by Raymond Lecoq, in his *Les Objets de la Vie Domestique,* Berger-Levrault, 1979. He also illustrates the *"roulette double"*, Plate **97** right, which may also be of French origin.

Note: Most metal jiggers are the work of founders, cast in non-ferrous metals, usually copper alloys, the majority of which are in brass, a few in bronze. Wrought iron requires different skills, those of the smith, and iron jiggers are much rarer. Cut steel, as in the case of the two jiggers right, **95** and **97** is even rarer.

95 A rare steel jigger, 19th century. 105mm.

MF 028

96 An iron jigger, 18th century, possibly Pennsylvanian German, its cutter resembling a whale's tail. 105mm.

MF 233

97 A finely-made all-steel double-wheeled jigger, 18th century. The upper wheel is cut to produce a conventional jagged edge while the lower cuts a continuous edge of Cs, probably French. 145mm.

MF 079

Pastry Jiggers and Pastry Prints

98 A rare iron-stemmed jigger with two brass wheels, each cutting a jagged edge, in differing sizes, 18th century, probably French. 170mm.
MF 052

99 A cast brass two-wheeled jigger, of Czechoslovakian origin, 18th century. 123mm.
MF 065

100 A cast brass two-wheeled jigger, the lathe-turned dished wheels of plain design, Eastern European, 18th century. 117mm.
MF 161

101 A two-wheeled brass jigger, the lower wheel with plain cutting edge, gilt-lacquered, of Canadian origin, 19th century. 115mm.
MF 062

102 A brass two-wheeled jigger with iron sides and cowhorn scales, British Isles, 19th century. 170mm.
MF 063

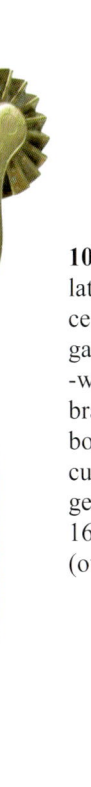

103 An 18th-century simple iron jigger with copper-alloy wheel, probably Pennsylvanian German. 175mm.
MF 239

104 A rare late 19th-century Hungarian double-wheeled brass jigger, one wheel of conventional jagging form, the other cutting a rectangular fret, the aluminium handle tang fitted with thermoplastic scales with copper rivets. 134mm long (overall).
MF 229

105 A rare late 18th-century Hungarian double-wheeled brass jigger, both wheels cutting a jagged edge. 167mm long (overall).
MF 187

Pastry Jiggers and Pastry Prints

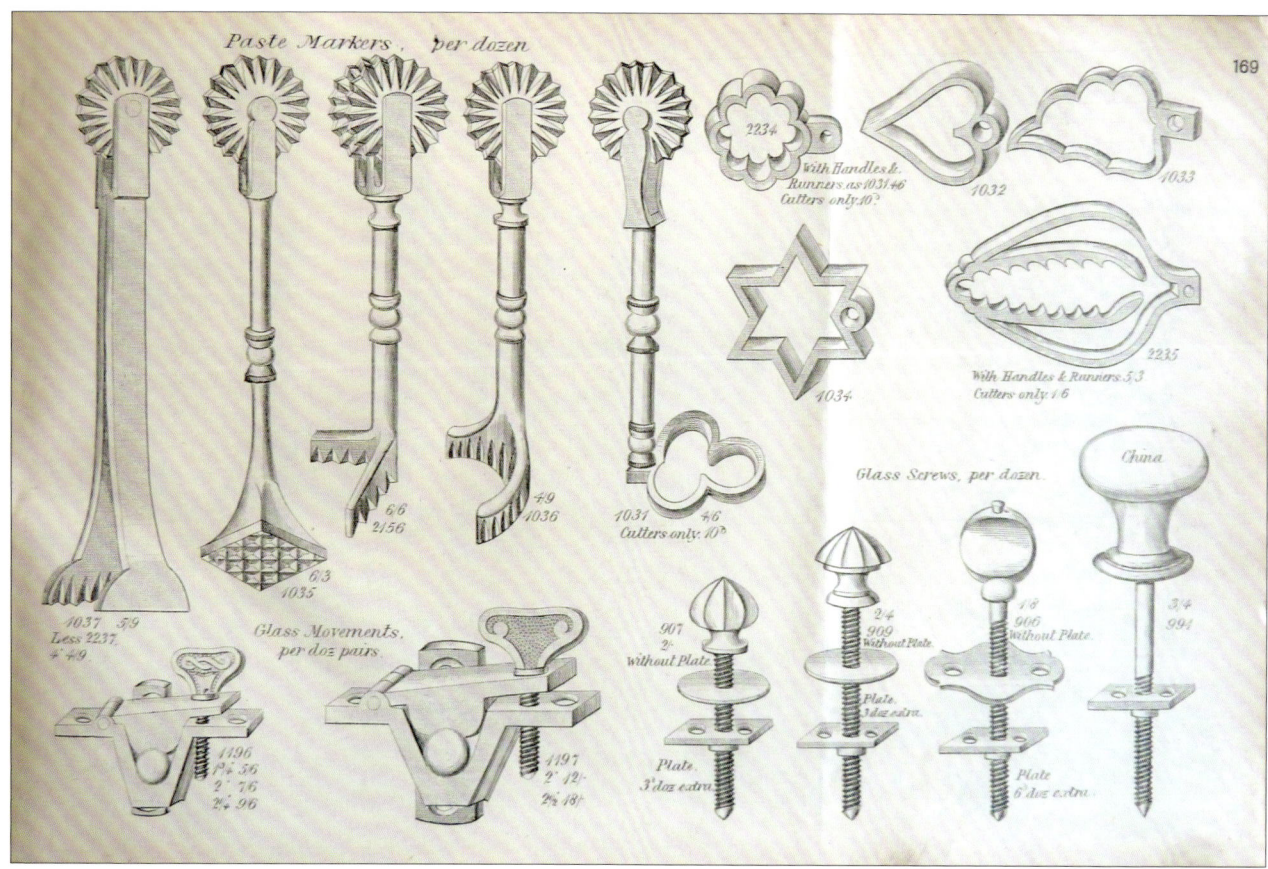

106 Page from a trade catalogue of "HHE" (probably Huxley), late 19th century. While the brass jiggers below are all very similar to those of the catalogue, all have minor differences of wheel cutting or stem decoration.

Courtesy Roderick Butler

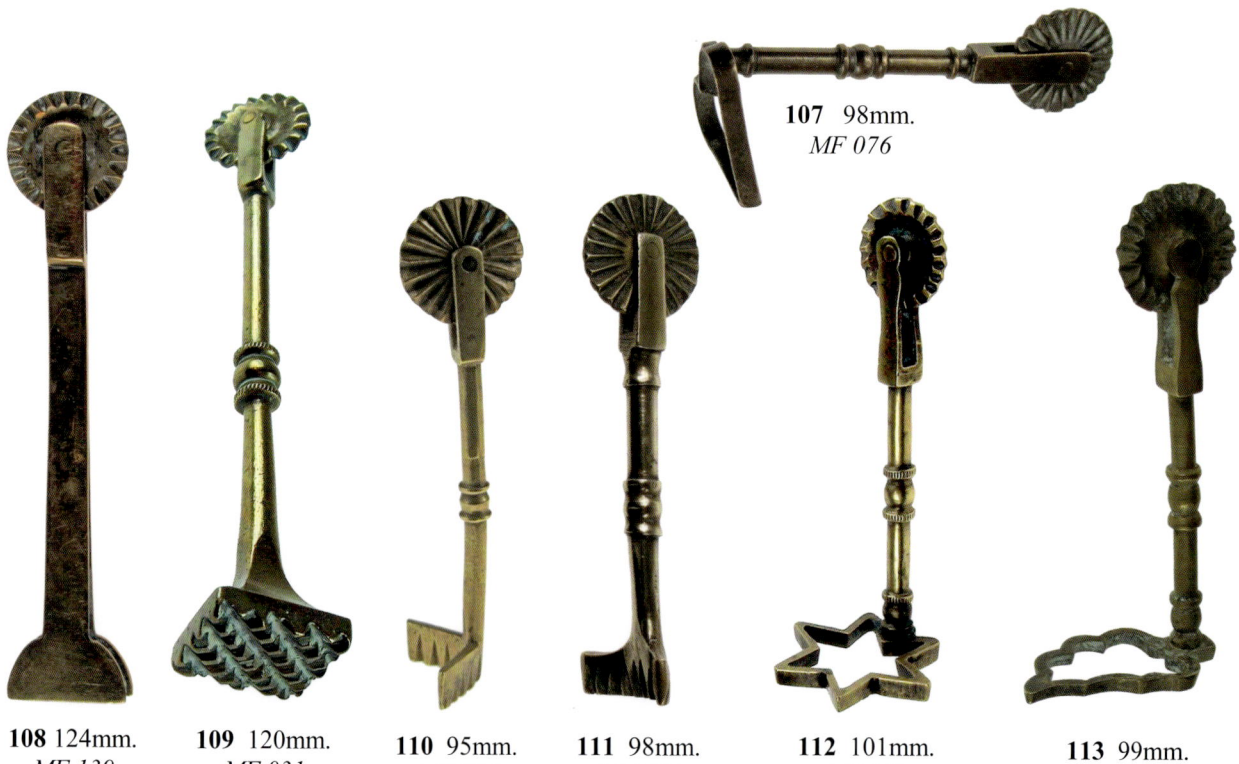

107 98mm. MF 076

108 124mm. MF 139

109 120mm. MF 031

110 95mm. MF 004

111 98mm. MF 071

112 101mm. MF 003

113 99mm. MF 163

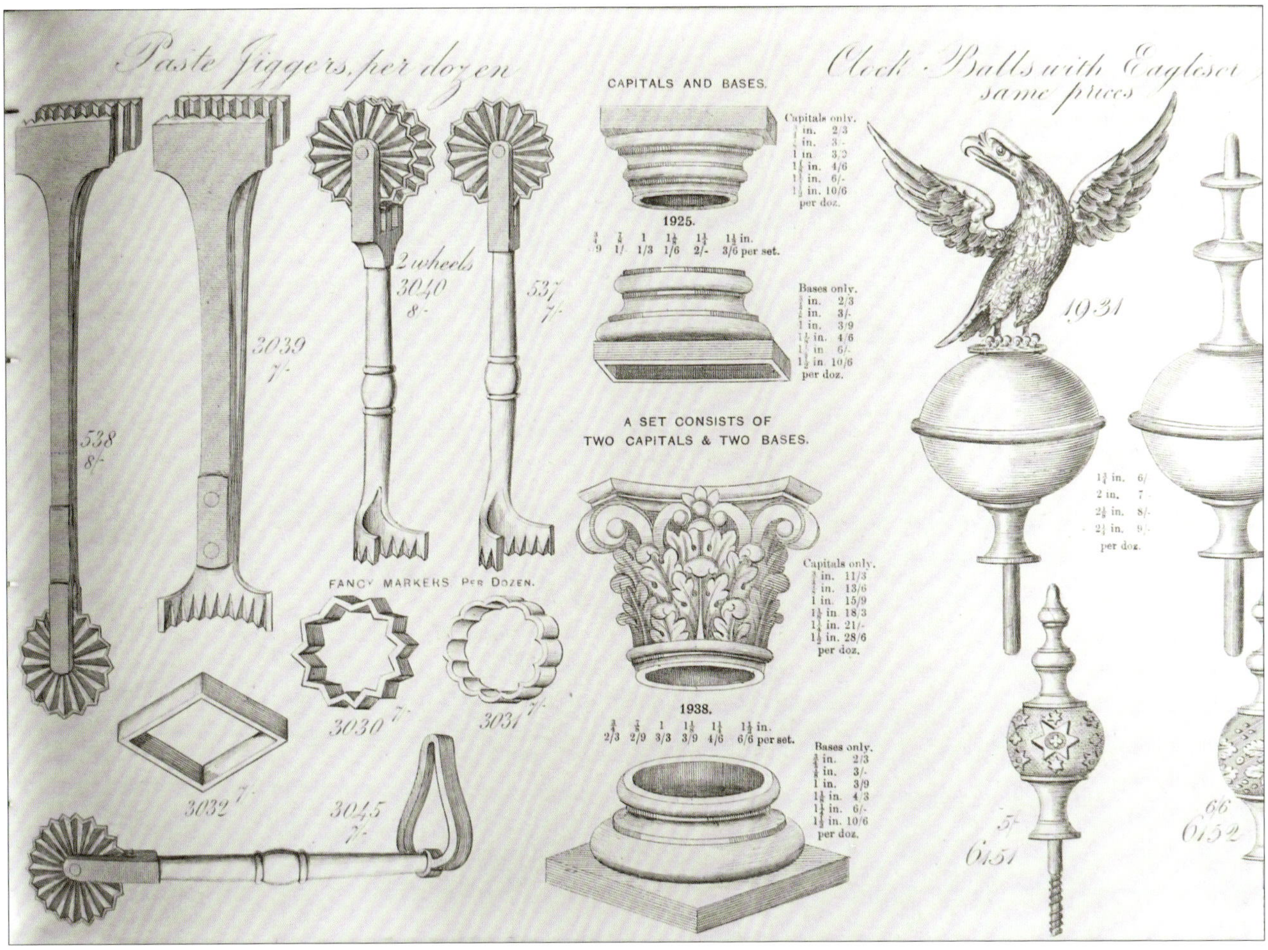

114 Trade catalogue of James Cartland & Sons, 1894. *Courtesy Roderick Butler*

The James Cartland & Sons' 1894 trade catalogue above uses some of the same engravings of jiggers as did the same firm's catalogue of 1878, (a copy of which is also in the Roderick Butler Collection), and interestingly, in the days of non-inflation, at the same prices. The author has not yet seen an example of any of the "Fancy Markers". These fancy markers seem to serve the same function as the "cutters" of the HHE catalogue opposite, which were patently sold with or without the jigger handles and wheel. In use they would certainly very readily cut through the pastry completely rather than merely impress it with their designs.

In spite of examining many examples of jiggers similar to those in contemporary catalogues, exact matches are very difficult to find, as will be seen from the examples illustrated left, from the author's collection. In many cases similar jiggers are found whose manufacture may have continued over many decades. This firm of brass founders was in business in Birmingham from before 1823 until 1955.

115 130mm. *MF 059*
116 111mm. *MF 162*
117 125mm. *MF 002*
118 110mm. *MF 166*

Pastry Jiggers and Pastry Prints

119 - 123 Five jiggers of the type which were offered in the late 19th century with alternative shape cutters, which could be purchased with or without the wheel and stem attachment, which screws on. Each is 111mm. Most jiggers of this type, including those with a knurled knop, as below, which appear in the HHE catalogue on page 26 have been permanently fixed by peening over the end of the stem.

MF 235, 234, 068, 073, 029

124 A brass jigger with maple-leaf-shaped cutter from the same foundry as those in Plates **119 - 123** above, but with fixed peened-over cutter, second half 19th century. 111mm.
MF 067
Note also the variation in wheel dentation with *MF 235* above.

125 - 127 Three brass jiggers with shape cutters, all no doubt made by the same firm of brass-founders, using a distinctive four-element knop, second half 19th century. 104, 100, 103mm.
MF 096, 238, 027

128 A late 19th-century brass jigger with knopped stem and incurved forks as in the HHE trade catalogue. (page 26), the shape-cutter based on the St. Edward's crown, perhaps for the 1887 or 1897 Jubilee. 98mm.
MF 053

Pastry Jiggers and Pastry Prints

129 A rare late Georgian brass pastry jigger with leaf-shaped cutter, the wheel having an edge made up of hollow-domed cups which when rolled under pressure create a line of beading, the whole of superior quality, early 19th century or perhaps slightly earlier. 110mm.

MF 077

130 A brass jigger with thistle-shaped cutter, late 19th century. 114mm. *Photograph the author, courtesy Ivan Day Collection*

131 A brass jigger with heart-shaped cutter, second half 19th century. 104mm.

MF 018

132 A brass jigger with daisy-shaped cutter, late 19th century. 120mm. *Photograph the author, courtesy Ivan Day Collection*

133 A brass jigger with lozenge-form cutter, late 19th century. 102mm.

MF 226

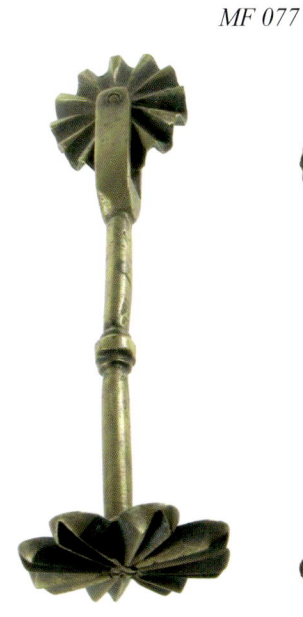

134 A brass jigger with a large octofoil floral print, early 19th century. 110mm.

MF 019

135 An unusual brass jigger with horizontal cutter of six-spoked wheel form, early 19th century. 96mm.

MF 115

136 A brass jigger with chequered print of gingerbread-man form, early 19th century. 93mm.

MF 025

137 A brass jigger with simple leaf cutter, late 19th century. 96mm.

MF 218

138 A brass jigger with leaf-shaped cutter, early 19th century. 106mm.

MF 016

29

Pastry Jiggers and Pastry Prints

141mm.	143mm.	144mm.	150mm.
MF 084	MF 086	MF 087	MF 097

139 - 142 Four rare mid to late 18th-century iron jiggers with cutting wheels to one end and tweezer-like crimpers to the other.

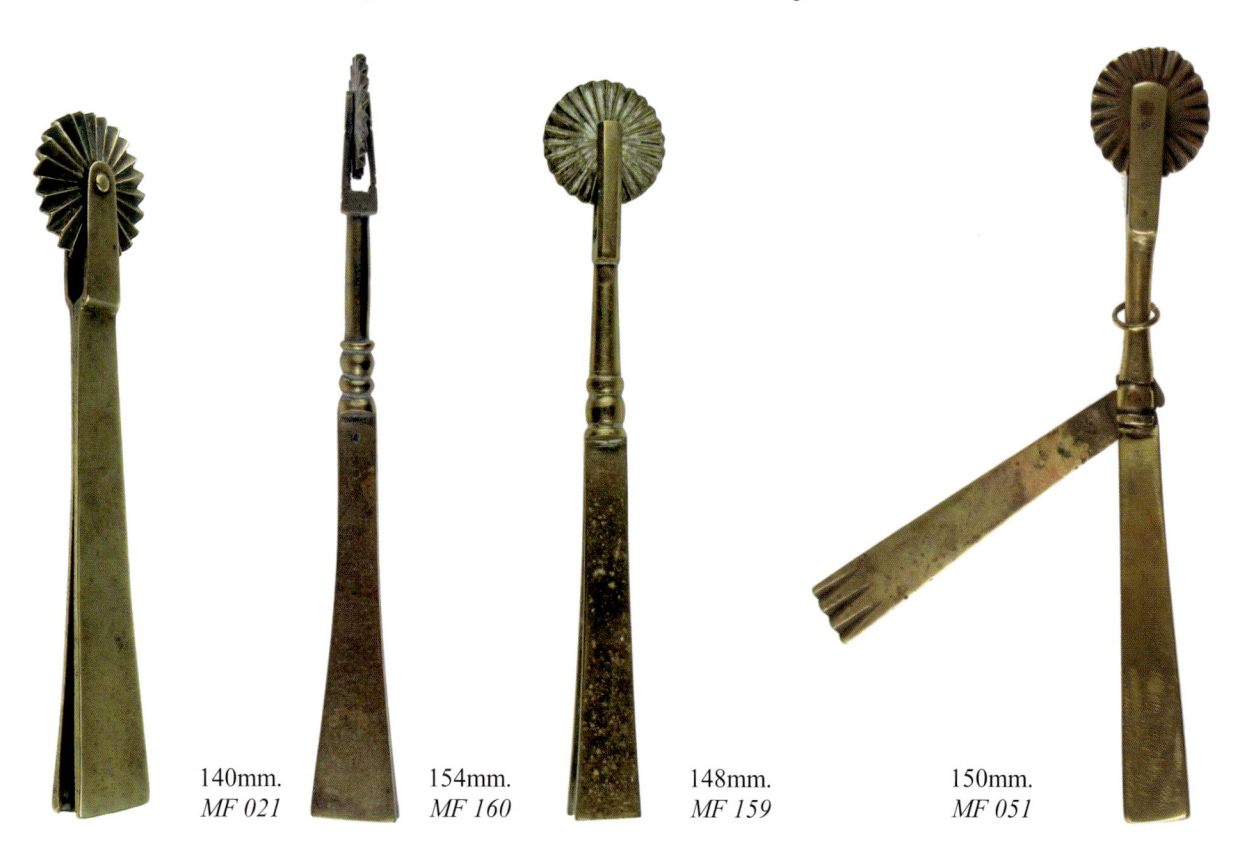

140mm.	154mm.	148mm.	150mm.
MF 021	MF 160	MF 159	MF 051

143 - 145 Three brass examples. These appear in trade catalogues of the late 18th and early 19th centuries.

146 A rare brass jigger with folding crimper to allow ease of cleaning after use. The locking ring is a replacement.

Pastry Jiggers and Pastry Prints

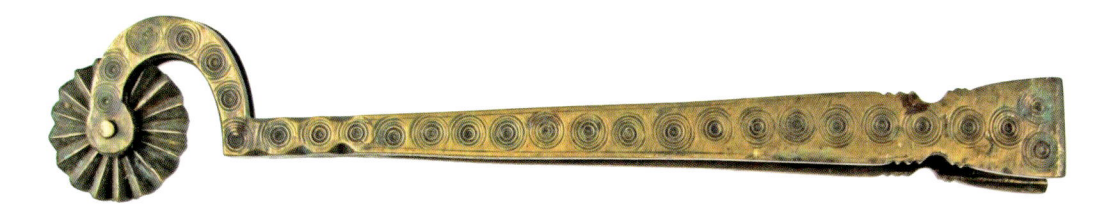

147 A very fine large brass jigger with finely shaped Baroque-style crimper and punched roundel decoration, late 17th/early 18th century. 192mm.

MF 072

138mm.	140mm.	147mm.	142mm.	142mm.	120mm.	113mm.	116mm.
MF 157	MF 213	MF 099	MF 058	MF 092	MF 060	MF 070	MF 128

148 - 155 A group of 18th- and 19th-century brass jiggers with crimpers. These were made over an extensive period, probably into the early 20th century.

156 A very rare jigger with an arced cutter/marker to one end and crimpers to the other, probably of the late 19th century when similar devices appear in trade catalogues, (See page 27 for such a catalogue).

This example has been later dismantled, fitted with a piece of clock mainspring and re-riveted using the original rivet holes, a considerable design improvement. 116mm.

MF 162

Pastry Jiggers and Pastry Prints

| 160mm. | 154mm. | 133mm. | | 129mm. | 139mm. | 147mm. |
| MF 036 | MF 208 | MF 059 | | MF 137 | MF 069 | MF 127 |

(Detail) An unusual crimper, with grips of shallow S-curve form. 138mm *MF 201*

| 108mm. | 124mm. | 130mm. | | 117mm. | 115mm. | 133mm. |
| MF 185 | MF 139 | MF 156 | | MF 113 | MF 136 | MF 093 |

157 - 169 A group of 19th-century brass jiggers with crimpers of different sizes and shapes. Similar jiggers appear in late 18th-century trade catalogue and were still being offered a century later.

Pastry Jiggers and Pastry Prints

170 A superb and very rare steel and copper-alloy jigger with cutting wheel and four prints of circular, square, lozenge and heart shapes, circa 1820. 200mm.
© *Courtesy Eve Stone Antiques*

Pastry Jiggers and Pastry Prints

171 A copper-alloy jigger with cutting wheel and two prints, one of lozenge shape, the other circular, with turned ebonised hardwood handle and ring suspender, early 19th century. 195mm.

MF 005

172 A copper-alloy jigger of uncommon form, with cutting wheel and single print of square shape, with turned ebonised hardwood handle, early 19th century. 180mm.

MF 010

173 A copper-alloy jigger with cutting wheel and two prints, one of lozenge shape, the other circular, with turned ebonised hardwood handle, early 19th century. 235mm.

MF 055

Pastry Jiggers and Pastry Prints

174 A copper-alloy jigger with cutting wheel and two prints, one of square shape, the other circular, with turned boxwood handle and ring suspender, early 19th century. 230mm.

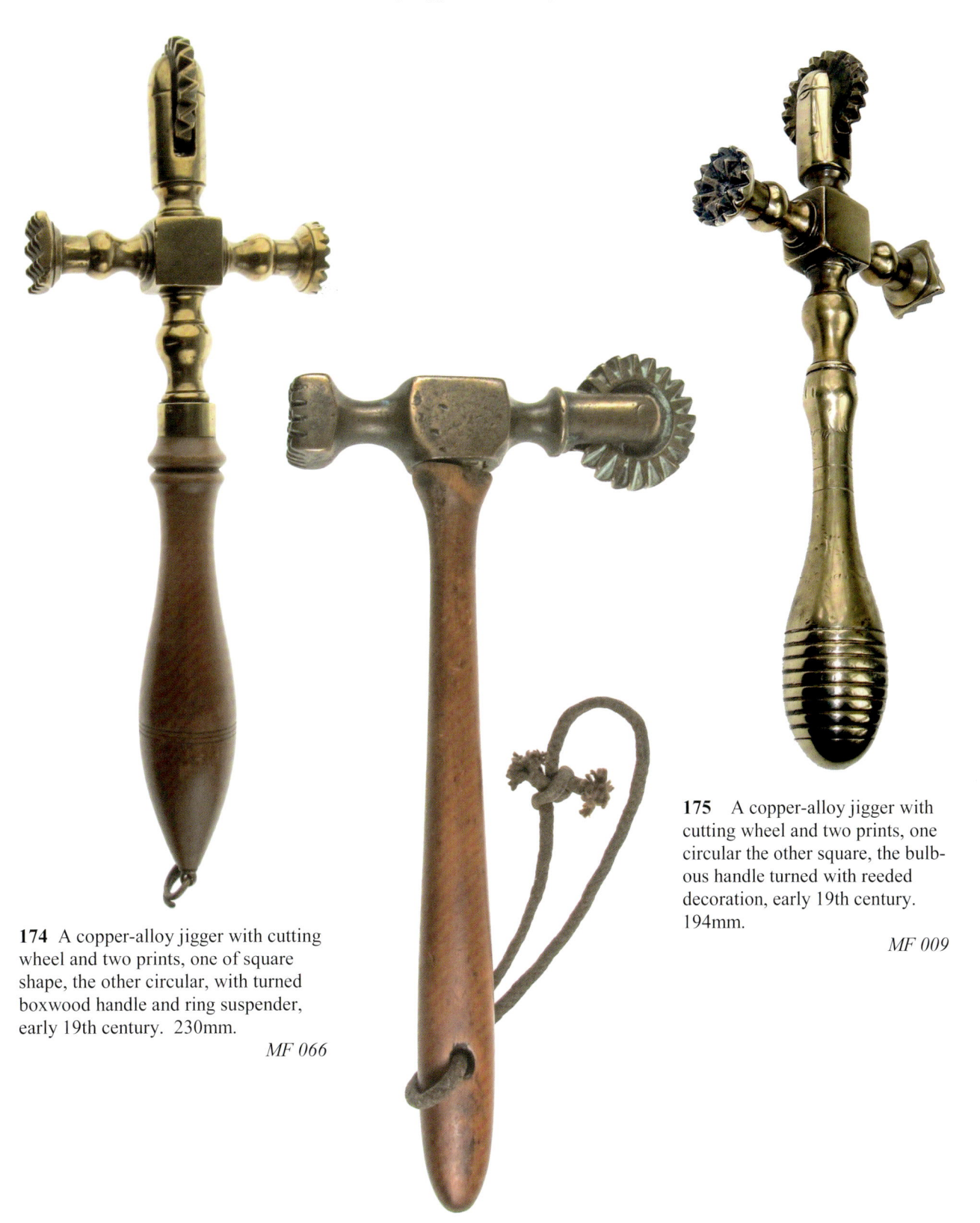

MF 066

175 A copper-alloy jigger with cutting wheel and two prints, one circular the other square, the bulbous handle turned with reeded decoration, early 19th century. 194mm.

MF 009

176 A copper-alloy jigger with cutting wheel and single square print, with shaped pearwood handle, pierced for cord suspension, early 19th century. 223 mm.

MF 102

35

Pastry Jiggers and Pastry Prints

177 Crathes Castle, Banchory, Aberdeenshire, a 16th-century tower house with later additions. Set in 240 hectares of formal gardens, woodland walks and rolling countryside, the house is administered by the National Trust for Scotland.

© Shutterstock.com

178 The 19th-century kitchen at Crathes Castle, the original home of this pastry jigger, with contemporary range and cast-iron cooking pots. On the table is a ridged rolling pin designed to crush oats.

© Courtesy National Trust for Scotland

179 A copper-alloy jigger with cutting wheel and two prints, one of lozenge shape, the other circular, the cross bar stamped "CRATHES CASTLE," with turned ebonised hardwood handle, early 19th century. 208mm.
MF 240

36

180 A copper-alloy jigger with cutting wheel and two prints, one of lozenge shape, the other circular, with turned ebonised hardwood handle, early 19th century. 171mm.

MF 183

181 A rare copper-alloy jigger with cutting wheel and two prints, one of lozenge shape, the other circular, with lemon-squeezer handle, treated to resemble gilt, early 19th century. 210mm.

Courtesy Julia Gant

182 A copper-alloy jigger with cutting wheel and two prints, one of square shape, the other circular, with turned beechwood handle, early 19th century. 236mm.

MF 241

Pastry Jiggers and Pastry Prints

183 A square brass print and double-balustroid stem with turned ebonised pearwood handle, c. 1820. 130mm.
MF 158

184 A square print, the bronze balustroid stem having a steel handle finial, c. 1820. 122mm.
MF 199

185 A square copper-alloy print with inverted balustroid stem and turned stained ash handle, c. 1820. 130mm.
MF 014

186 A square bronze print, with balustroid stem and mushroom-style finial, c. 1820. 105mm.
MF 216

187 A square copper-alloy print with knopped stem and turned boxwood handle, c. 1820. 130mm.
MF 012

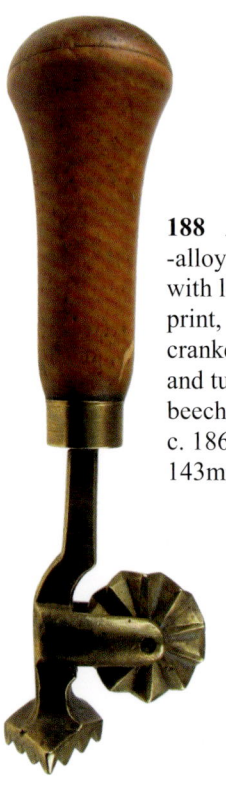

188 A copper-alloy jigger with lozenge print, on cranked stem and turned beech handle, c. 1860. 143mm.
MF 098

189 A copper-alloy print of square form, on double-balustroid stem with turned lignum vitae handle, c. 1820. 122mm.
MF 056

190 A copper-alloy print, of square form, with turned fruitwood handle, c. 1850. 125mm.
MF 191

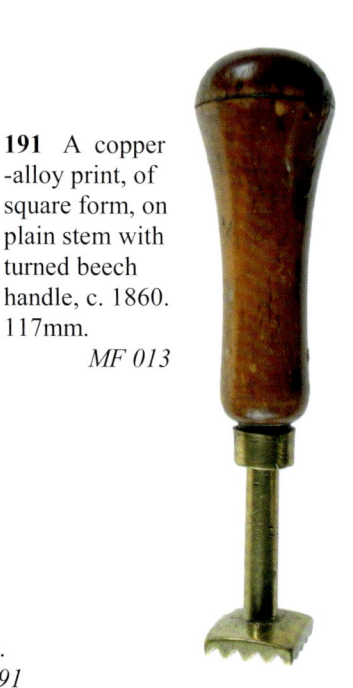

191 A copper-alloy print, of square form, on plain stem with turned beech handle, c. 1860. 117mm.
MF 013

38

Pastry Jiggers and Pastry Prints

192, 193 Two similar jiggers with square prints, on inverted balustroid stems, one of a bronze-like alloy, the other brass, c. 1820. 110mm.
MF 095, 017

194 An iron and copper-alloy jigger with spiked wheel and chequered circular print, early 18th Century. 124mm.
MF 118

195, 196 A copper-alloy jigger with lozenge print, on reel-knopped stem, mid to late 19th century, and another, brass, with knurled knop. 120mm.
MF 026, 031

197 A copper-alloy square print, on turned inverted balustroid stem with ovoid finial, late 18th century. 123mm.
MF 011

198 An all-steel square print, on turned stem with acorn finial, mid 18th century. 90mm.
MF 133

199 A lacquered brass jigger with circular print, on knopped stem, c. 1880. 100mm.
MF 032

200 A copper-alloy jigger with square print, plain stem and domed finial, early 19th century. 60mm.
MF 200

201 A steel pastry print, the turned treen handle with knurled brass ferrule, late 18th-century. 115mm.
Courtesy Edward Harrison Collection

Pastry Jiggers and Pastry Prints

203 A rudely-made copper-alloy pastry wheel, probably from a coin, with brass supports, lacking its wooden handle. 105 mm.
MF 171

202 Pastry jigger with wheel made from a USA copper Large Cent of circa 1854, with plain deal handle and wrought-iron wheel-holder.
Courtesy Carole Holt
www.carolescountry.com

204 and details A wrought-iron jigger with copper wheel fashioned from a Canadian One Penny (Two Sous) Bank Token of 1852, 140mm long. An example of the host coin in good condition is also shown.
Photographs courtesy Carl J. Davis Collection

205 Two examples of the use of redundant copper coins to cut pastry jigger wheels, USA Large Cents of 1842 and 1854.
Courtesy Gary Hahn
www.early-copper.com

40

Pastry Jiggers and Pastry Prints

206 A love-token bone double-wheeled pastry jigger, engraved "Mrs Nicholls", an example of late Georgian folk art. Sold by Andrew Smith & Sons, Auctioneers, Itchen Stoke, 5the July, 2011, Lot 936.
Courtesy, Gary Loftus

207 and detail below A rare American wrought-iron pastry jigger, its wheel made from an Italian States (Naples and Sicily) copper 5-Tornesi coin, of 1798. This pre-Unification of Italy state issue was coined only for the years 1797 and 1798. 146mm.
Photograph courtesy Carl J. Davis Collection

208 A second-half 19th-century pastry jigger with wheel fashioned from a USA Large Cent of 1850, with plain tapering wrought-iron handle. 156mm.
Photograph Courtesy Carl J. Davis Collection

209 and detail. A second-half 19th-century pastry jigger with simple treen, possibly cedar, handle, the wheel made from a USA Braided Hair Cent coin of 1843. 157mm.
Photographs courtesy Carl J. Davis Collection

210 Pastry jigger with wheel fashioned from a George III copper penny struck at Matthew Boulton's Soho Mint, in Birmingham, England, in 1806, and naturally-bent hardwood handle, probably mid 19th century.
Courtesy Carole Holt
www.carolescountry.com

41

Pastry Jiggers and Pastry Prints

211 A rare if somewhat rudely fashioned blacksmith-made wrought iron jigger of large size, American, 18th or 19th century. 229mm.

MF 147

212 An early 19th-century pastry jigger, the copper-alloy wheel having wrought-iron supports, the handle of helically-fluted bronze. 173mm.

Photograph courtesy Carl J. Davis Collection

213 A primitive Slovenian home-made jigger with brass wheel and oak handle, 19th century. 145mm.

MF 237

214 An extremely rare blacksmith-made wrought-iron jigger, probably 18th century. 129mm.

MF 085

215 A German jigger with copper-alloy wheel, the handle improvised from a redundant 18th-century key. 109mm.

MF 198

216 A rare wrought-iron jigger of conventional form. 105mm.

MF 140

Pastry Jiggers and Pastry Prints

217 A 19th-century Hungarian jigger with copper-alloy wheel and hand-fashioned beech handle, varnished; folk art with a very sculptural quality. 150mm.

MF 148

218 Another 19th-century Hungarian jigger with a copper wheel and carved black walnut handle of high quality. 150mm.

MF 152

219 A plainer Hungarian jigger with sycamore handle and iron wheel. 155mm.

MF 151

220 An elegantly carved wooden jigger with a complex edge pattern to the wheel, Pennsylvanian German, early 19th Century. 162mm.

MF 104

221 A simple and purely functional 19th-century Hungarian jigger with turned sycamore handle and iron wheel. 156mm.

MF 153

222 A simply-made root walnut jigger, a pleasing example of folk art, probably made as a love token. 210mm.

MF 155

43

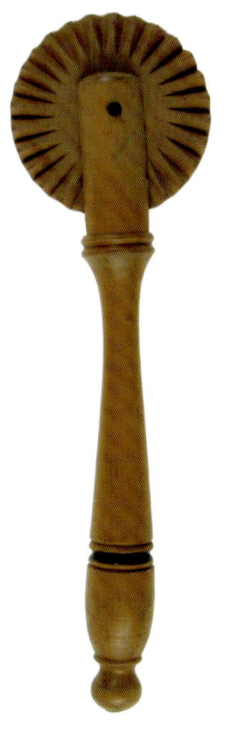

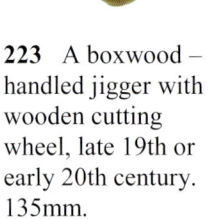

Pastry Jiggers and Pastry Prints

223 A boxwood – handled jigger with wooden cutting wheel, late 19th or early 20th century. 135mm.
MF 129

224 A fruitwood – handled jigger with bone cutting wheel, late 19th or early 20th century. 127mm.
MF 182

225 A simply turned and cheaply-made sycamore-handled jigger with bone cutting wheel, later fitted with a small hook for hanging, 20th century. 135mm excluding hook.
MF 094

226 A well-made turned pearwood jigger with bone cutting wheel, 19th or early 20th century. 120mm.
MF 006

227 a and b A pair of jiggers with finely turned boxwood handles and wooden cutting wheels, late 19th or early 20th century. 129mm.
MF 231/2

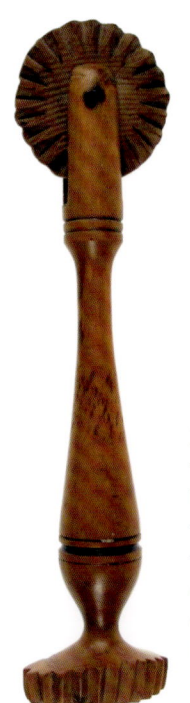

228 A rare jigger with finely turned boxwood handle, wooden cutting wheel and arced crimper, late 19th or early 20th century. 140mm.
MF 109

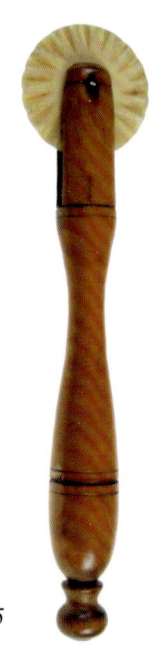

229 A high-quality boxwood-handled jigger with bone cutting wheel, late 19th or early 20th century. 122mm.
MF 075

Pastry Jiggers and Pastry Prints

230 A large turned sycamore jigger with a white opaline glass cutting wheel, mid to late 19th century, the wheel with contemporary glued repair; obviously a humble but valued possession. 180mm.
MF 107

231 A fine sycamore-handled jigger with a white porcelain cutting wheel painted in underglaze blue with a floral design, somewhat similar to the Meissen onion-flower pattern, Austrian or German, late 19th century. 203mm.
MF 132

232 Another sycamore-handled jigger with a white porcelain cutting wheel, decorated with Limoges-style polychrome forget-me-nots and gilt enrichment, Austrian or German, late 19th century. 215mm.
MF 134

233 Another sycamore-handled jigger with a white porcelain cutting wheel, decorated in the Viennese Secessionist style with gilding and printed rose panels, Austrian or German, late 19th century. 215mm.
MF 210

234 An oak-handled jigger with iron supports to the white opaline glass cutting wheel, German, mid 19th century. 203mm.
MF 116

Pastry Jiggers and Pastry Prints

235 A brass pastry-cutting wheel with turned sycamore handle, German, 19th century. 165mm.
MF 061

236 An unusual pastry jigger with copper-alloy wheel of industrial size, stamped with the orb-and-cross maker's mark of Benham and Froud of London, with turned sycamore handle, mid 19th century. 165 mm.
MF 108

Benham and Froud took over the firm started in 1785 by John Kepp, a coppersmith and brazier, in Chandos Street, London. In 1821, under the ownership of Richard and Edward Kepp, the firm made the replacement orb and cross for St. Paul's cathedral, 23 feet high and weighing seven tons. Benham and Froud took over the firm in 1855, adopted the symbol as their trademark, and used it from that time until 1924.

Source: www.oldcopper.org, quoting John Hardcastle.

237 A brass pastry-cutting wheel with turned sycamore handle, German, late 18th or early 19th century. 150mm.
MF 106

238 A fine late 18th–/early 19th-century pastry jigger with chamfered iron shank, brass wheel and well-patinated ash handle, American. 213 mm.
MF 101

46

Pastry Jiggers and Pastry Prints

239 A pastry jigger, the copper–alloy wheel cutting a series of semi-circular arcs, with turned fruitwood handle, French, early 19th century. 167mm.
MF 169

240 A small brass pastry jigger, possibly for a child, with turned rosewood handle, early 19th century. 108mm.
MF 196

241 A steel pastry-cutting wheel *(roulette coupé pâte)* with tapering knopped stem and stained boxwood handle, French, 18th century. 162mm.
MF 121

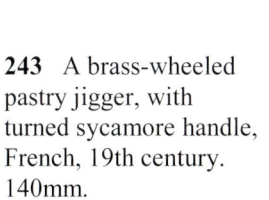

242 A well-finished pastry jigger, the brass stem having knurled decoration, with turned beech handle, early 19th century. 189mm.
MF 125

243 A brass-wheeled pastry jigger, with turned sycamore handle, French, 19th century. 140mm.
MF 120

244 A cheaply-made pastry jigger, with brass wheel, iron ferrule and turned beech handle, late 19th or early 20th century. 180mm.
MF 189

Pastry Jiggers and Pastry Prints

245 A brass and turned beech jigger, German, 19th century. 133mm.
MF 205

246 A brass and turned beech jigger, German, 19th century. 170mm.
MF 203

247 An opaline glass and turned sycamore jigger, German, 19th century. 168mm.
MF 219

248 A brass and turned beech jigger, German, 19th century. 198mm.
MF 204

249 An iron jigger, late 19th century. 180mm.
MF 194

250 A Piedmontese brass and turned beech filled-pasta cutter with jigger edge, 20th century. 85mm high.
MF 217

251 A Piedmontese brass filled-pasta cutter with jigger edge, 19th century. 69mm high.
MF 209

252 A Piedmontese brass and turned beech filled-pasta cutter with jigger edge, early 20th century. 85mm high.
Courtesy Ivan Day Collection

Pastry Jiggers and Pastry Prints

253 A !9th-century Swedish cast-brass jigger, retaining the file marks of hand-finishing. 165mm long (overall).
MF 146

254 A 19th-century Swedish cast-brass jigger, the shank rudely decorated with a continuous lozenge design, the surface "pickled" to simulate gilding. 157mm long (overall).
MF 220

255 A !9th-century Swedish cast-brass jigger, cast with a lozenge design, retaining the file marks of hand-finishing. 148mm long (overall).
MF 236

256 A 19th-century Swedish cast-brass jigger, the shank having continuous scrolling foliate decoration. 165mm long (overall).
MF 197

Swedish cast brass jiggers of this type were made from the early nineteenth century and exported throughout Scandinavia and the Baltic countries until at least the mid twentieth century, freight costs, tolls and excise duties minimised by the reduction in weight achieved by their piercings. A wood-and-clay moulding box to cast eight examples of the shank of such a jigger, with an inventory mark dated 1883, was offered for sale at a fair in Uppsala some years ago. *(Ex. Inf.* Renato Rabiotti*)*

257, 258 Two German brass jiggers, each with two wheels varying in design, 19th century. 114mm and 120 long (overall). These too have piercings to economise on the amount of metals used to make them, and in terms of freight charges, etc.
MF 227, 193

49

259 Lechner & Stump's patent "Combination Pie Rimmer, Crimper and Pastry Cutter", patented September 11th, 1866 and sold for 50 cents. The slightly modified example above is stamped with this patent date. 147mm.

MF 100

260 Advertising broadsheet for the Lechner & Stump device above. 355 x 182mm.

MF Collection

Dealers in Patent Rights,
LOOK TO YOUR INTERESTS!

Buy LECHNER & STUMP'S CELEBRATED COMBINATION PATENT PIE RIMMER, CRIMPER AND PASTRY CUTTER, an article of absolute utility in every household. Patented Sept. 11, 1866. It is an invaluable addition to the Pastry.

BAKING MADE EASY.

Every family in the United States ought to have one. It cuts off the dough around the edge of the pie plate, ornaments it with a neat fringe-like appearance, and at the same time presses the upper and lower crust of the pie firmly together. Warranted not to let out the juice from the pie—which is often very annoying. It consists of a rotary cutter and ornamental roller or crimper attached, in combination with a small corrugated wheel or pastry cutter to one end of a handle, having a butter cutter or print formed upon the othe end. The annexed drawing will give a perfect idea of the workings and looks of the machine, which will enable the most inexperienced to use to perfection and convince the most skeptical of its utility and economy. The enviable reputation it has already achieved invites comparison and defies competition. Its neat-like appearance will make it an ornament to the household of the richest, and its low retail price of 50 cents will bring it within the reach of the poorest families.

Buy no other until you have seen the Combination Pie Rimmer, Crimper and Pastry Cutter.
Agents wanted in every town and county throughout the United States.
State and County Rights for sale on reasonable terms.
For further particulars apply to proprietors,

LECHNER & STUMP,
Sheridan, Pa.

Travelling Agent for

Pastry Jiggers and Pastry Prints

261 A mid 20th-century aluminium jigger, stamped "CHIARUGI BROS. MFG. CHICAGO. ILL.", the handle cast in a two-piece mould. The firm was founded in the 1920s, and is still in business, as Chiarugi Hardware, at 1412 West Taylor Street, Chicago, the present owner having purchased the firm in 1965.
MF 167

262 Anonymous mid to late 20th-century jigger with white plastic crimper and stained hardwood handle. 182mm.
MF 124

263 Anonymous 20th-century cast aluminium jigger. 173mm.
MF 164

264 Unmarked 20th-century tinned-steel jigger. 160mm.
MF145

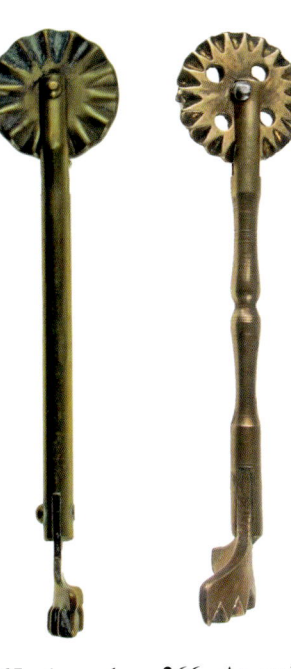

265 An early 20th-century cheaply-made brass jigger with tubular stem and riveted-on arced crimper. 125mm.
MF172

266 An early 20th-century cheaply-made bronze jigger with riveted-on arced crimper, stamped "GERMANY". 116mm.
MF 242

267 A cheaply-made jigger with iron wheel stamped "WESTERN IMPORTING CO., MINNEAPOLIS. MINN", the wooden handle painted black. 134mm.
Private Collection

268 An early 20th-century cast brass jigger stamped "BRITISH/MAKE". 103mm.
MF 168

269 A late 19th-/early 20th-century brass jigger, the stem stamped "GERMANY".
Private Collection

51

Pastry Jiggers and Pastry Prints

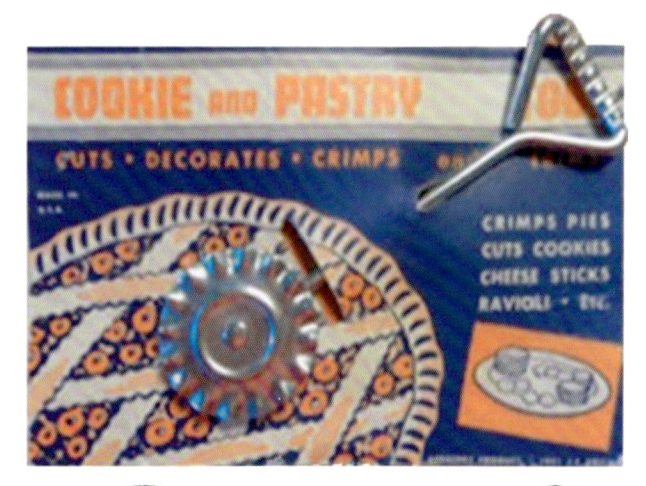

270 A 20th-century American mass-produced steel **"COOKIE AND PASTRY TOOL"** of simple but effective design. 115mm.

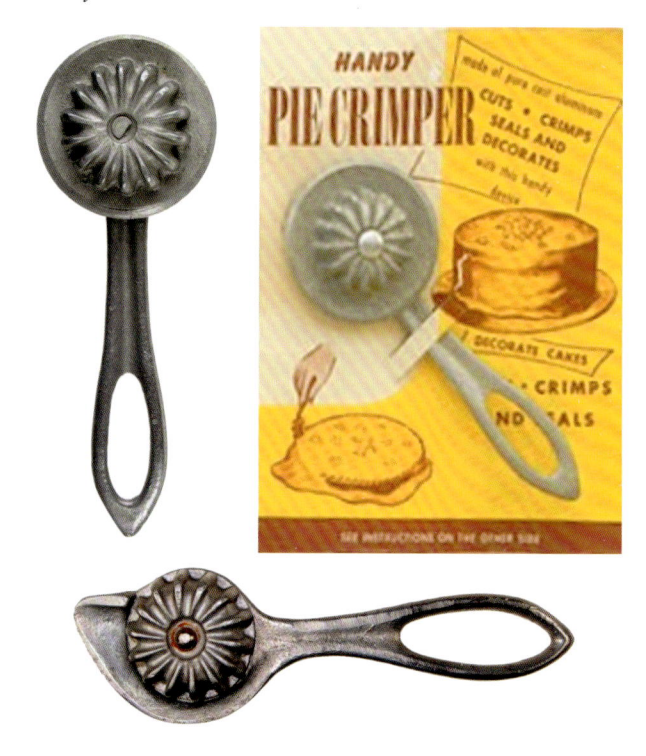

MF 144

271, 272 A 1930s cast aluminium **"HANDY PIE CRIMPER"**, 125mm, and below, another version. 129mm.

MF 142 and MF 143

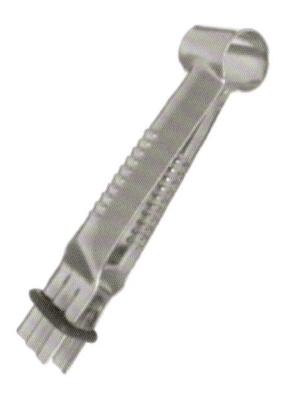

273 A modern (2013) French **"Scalloped PIE CRIMPER"** manufactured in China. 89mm.

MF149

Note its similarity of design and function with Scappi's *Molete per pasta* of 1570. (p. 10).

274 A modern (2013) American pastry jigger with stained turned wooden handle impressed **"CHICAGO METALLIC"** and chromium-plated steel crimping wheel. 165mm.

MF 150

Pastry Jiggers and Pastry Prints

275 A jigger by the Nutbrown Company of Walker Street, Blackpool, Design Registration No 812652, registered with the Board of Trade between March 28th and October 19th, 1936. The firm was taken over by Stephenson Mills, in 1969.

MF 228

276 The "DANDY" pastry jigger by Nutbrown Products, Patent 28th April, 1925, tin-plated steel, painted wooden handle, (available in several colours). 152mm.

MF 103

277 A modern jigger with stainless-steel wheel and lacquered painted wood handle. The firm of Taylor-Law & Co, trading as Tala, was founded in 1899 and now is one of many brands of kitchen equipment taken over by George East (Housewares), Ltd., of Leiston, Suffolk. This jigger was produced between 2000 and 2002.

MF 138

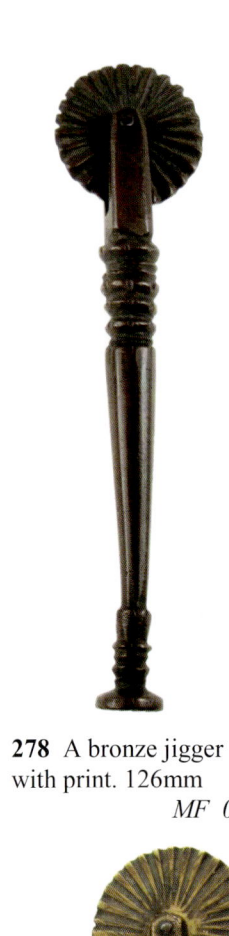

Pastry Jiggers and Pastry Prints

278 A bronze jigger with print. 126mm
MF 035

279 A simple bronze pastry wheel. 155mm
MF 044

280 A brass jigger with circular print. 160mm
MF 047

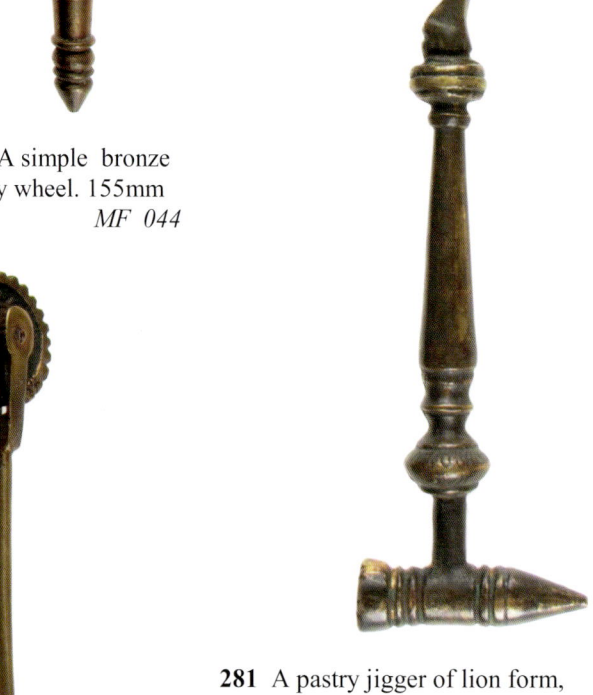

281 A pastry jigger of lion form, the bullet-like terminal possibly for breaking ice or toffee. 190mm
MF 050

282, 283 Two combination bronze spoons and pastry jiggers. 179 and 155mm
MF 038, 045

284 A pastry wheel with simple pricker terminal. 130mm
MF 040

Pastry Jiggers and Pastry Prints

285, 286 and detail Two similar Indian brass jiggers, decorated with parakeets, each 118mm,
MF 041, 046

These two jiggers are of Hindu origin, that on the right prick-engraved with an inscription in the Northern Indian script Devanagari which reads "Shri Lilavati (or Lalavata) Ma". Lilavati, "playful", is one of the more pleasant avatars of the somewhat fierce goddess Durga.*

The presence of such an invocation to a Hindu goddess, presumably to watch over the user and assist her or him to make better pastry, suggests that these Indian jiggers were used not only in the kitchens of members of the British Raj but also probably had a function in Indian domestic pastry-making.

* The author is indebted to Dr. Katherine Schofield of King's College, London, for this translation, and to Professor Rachel Cowgill of the University of Huddersfield for arranging this.

286, 287 Two similar Indian brass jiggers, each with a circular print. 143 and 133mm.
MF 043, 207

288 An unusual brass jigger decorated with a peacock, a bird much encountered in Hindu art. 135mm.
MF 042

Most of the Indian jiggers illustrated on these two pages date from the 19th century and were bought from Indian sources, with the exception of **287**, bought in England. That in Plate **278** may be earlier, perhaps 18th century.

289, 290 Two stylish and almost identical Indian brass jiggers each with a circular print. 145mm and 142mm.
MF 039, 048

55

RECIPES
mentioning jagging-irons, etc., and some productions using them

Pastry Jiggers and Pastry Prints

Jagging irons were not used exclusively for pastry. The recipe (right) in Richard Bradley's *The Country Housewife and Lady's Director,* of 1736, for example, requires its use for the fashioning of imitation cocks' combs from tripe.

291 Real cocks' combs. Fried like bacon, they were considered a delicacy.
Courtesy www.ideasinfood.typepad.com

Part II.   DIRECTOR.   79

To make artificial Coxcombs.   *From Mr.* Renaud.

TAKE Tripe, without any Fat, and with a sharp Knife pare away the fleshy part, leaving only the brawny or horny part about the thickness of a Cock's Comb. Then, with a Jagging-Iron, cut Pieces out of it, in the shape of Cocks Combs, and the remaining Parts between, may be cut to pieces, and used in Pyes, and serve every whit as well as Cocks Combs: but those cut in form, please the Eye best; and, as Mr. *Renaud* observes, the Eye must be pleased, before we can taste any thing with Pleasure. And therefore, in Fricassées we should put those which are cut according to Art.

292 A recipe calling for use of a jagging iron, 1736.
Photograph the author, courtesy Ivan Day Collection.

293 Artificial cocks' combs made by the author from tripe using this iron pastry wheel (jagging iron). An acquired taste, I think. To paraphrase James Woodforde, (Diary of a Country Parson, February 17th, 1763), "N.B. I shall not dine on roasted tongue and udder again very soon", *I shall not dine on artificial cocks' combs again very soon.*

294 An iron pastry jigger of heavy construction, 19th century. 190mm., used for this recipe
MF 202

57

Pastry Jiggers and Pastry Prints

295 A brass wheel-cutter with turned sycamore handle, mid 19th century. 170mm.
MF 181

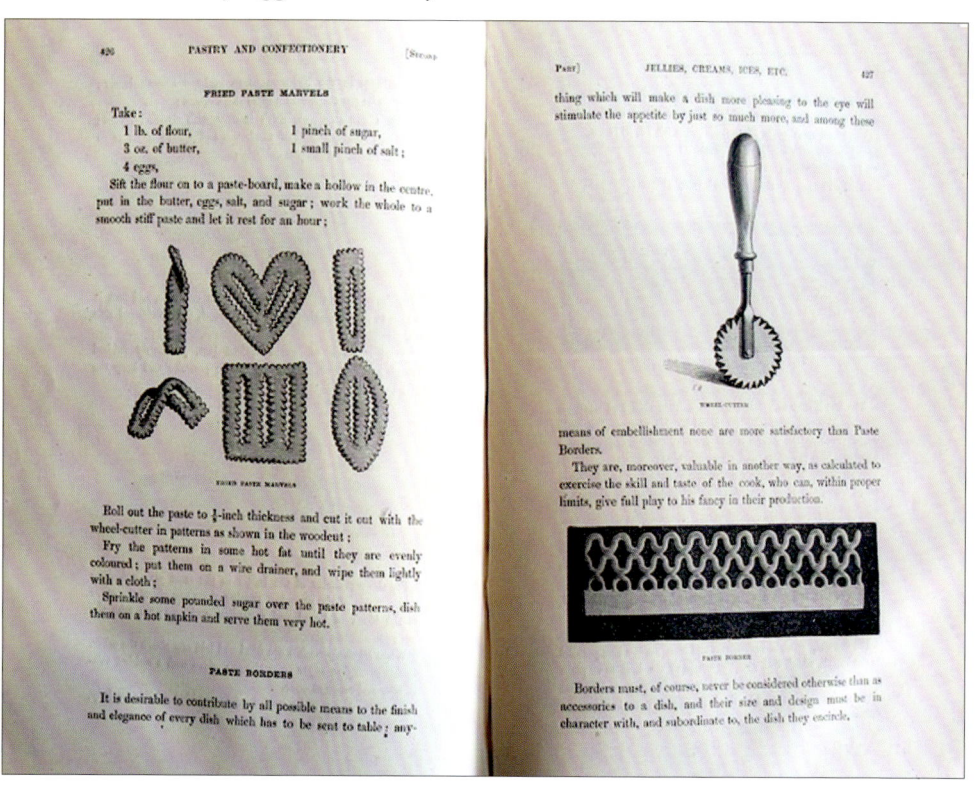

296 A recipe for "FRIED PASTE MARVELS" from Jules Goufé's *The Royal Book of Pastry and Confectionery*, London 1874, page 426, calling for the use of a "wheel cutter",.
Photograph, the author, courtesy the Ivan Day Collection.

297 "Fried paste marvels" made by the author using the recipe and pastry jigger above.

58

Pastry Jiggers and Pastry Prints

298 A recipe for "SMALL CAKES OF PUIS D'AMOUR" from Mr Borella's *The Court and Country Confectioner,* London, 1772, which calls for the component parts to be cut out with a "dented jagging iron". The Piedmontese filled-pasta cutters with dentate cutting edges work equally well. It is likely that "Puis d'amour" meaning "Then of Love" is a mistranscription of "PUITS D'AMOUR", "Wells of Love".

299 An Italian brass and wood pasta cutter with jagging edge, early 20th century. 85mm high.
MF 217

300 An iron ring cutter with jagging edge, early 20th century. 180mm.
MF 194

301 An Italian all-brass pasta cutter with jagging edge, mid 19th century. 69mm high,
MF 209

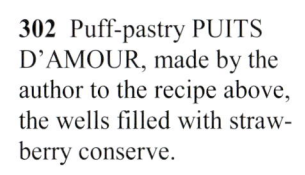

302 Puff-pastry PUITS D'AMOUR, made by the author to the recipe above, the wells filled with strawberry conserve.

59

Pastry Jiggers and Pastry Prints

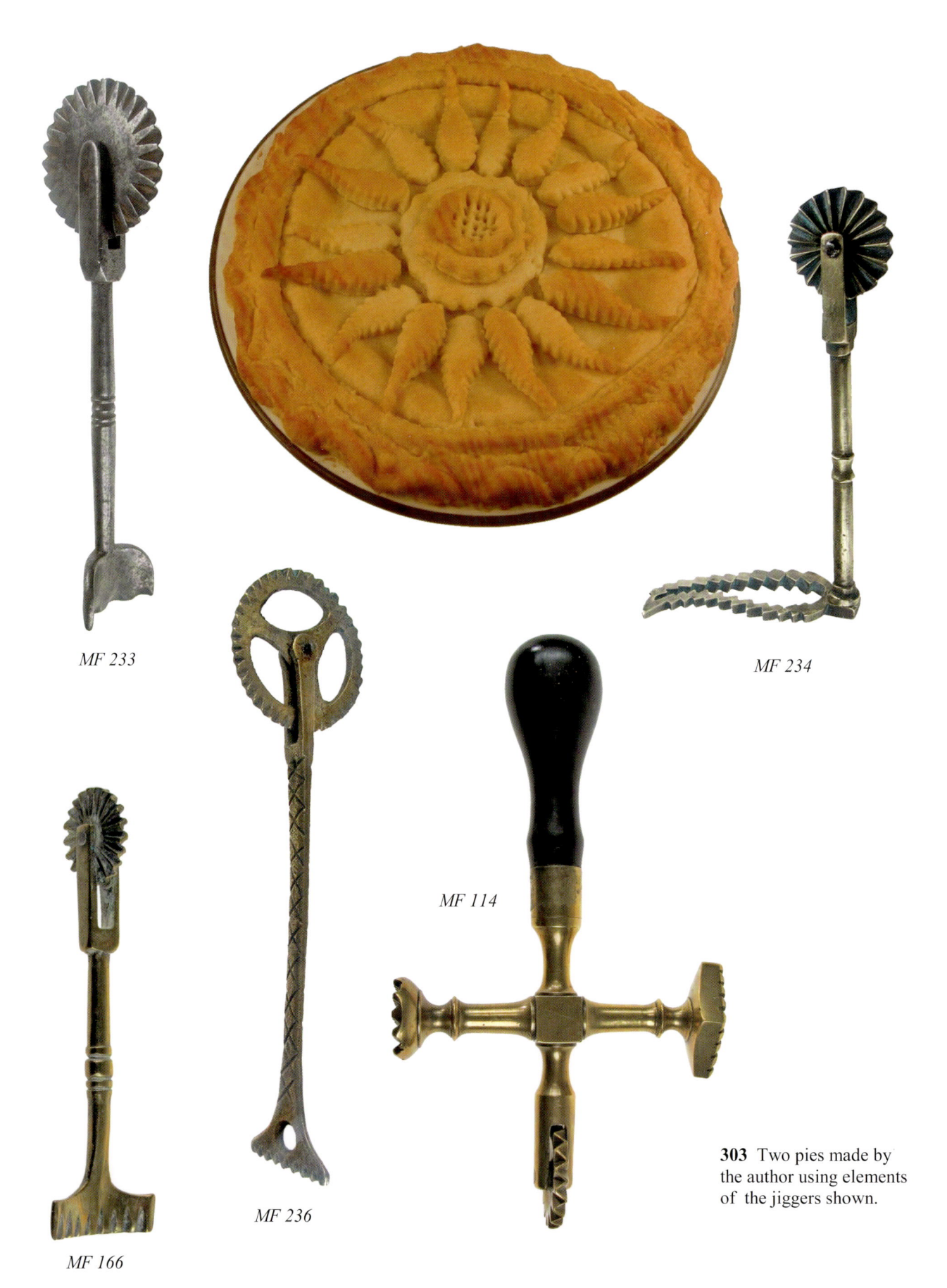

MF 233

MF 234

MF 166

MF 236

MF 114

303 Two pies made by the author using elements of the jiggers shown.

Pastry Jiggers and Pastry Prints

MF 202

MF 194

MF 077

MF 165

MF 212

MF 166

Pastry Jiggers and Pastry Prints

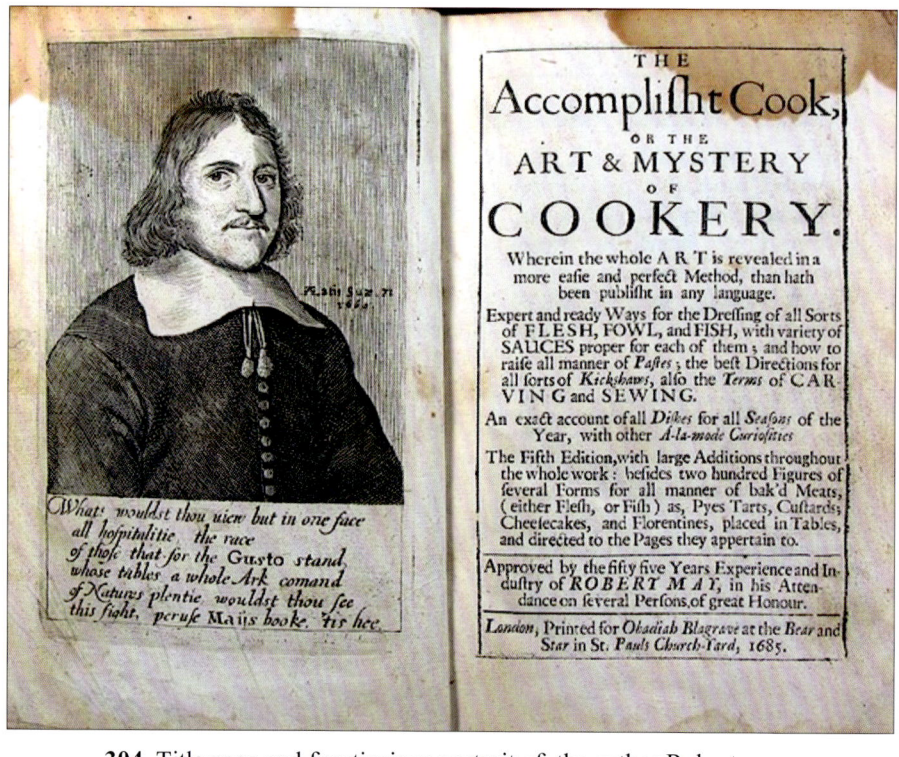

304 Title page and frontispiece portrait of the author Robert May, from his *The Accomplisht Cook or the Art & Mystery of Cookery,* London, 1685.

Photograph the author, courtesy Ivan Day

305 A brass jigger, the wheel with simple zig-zag cut, 19th century.
Photograph the author, courtesy Ivan Day

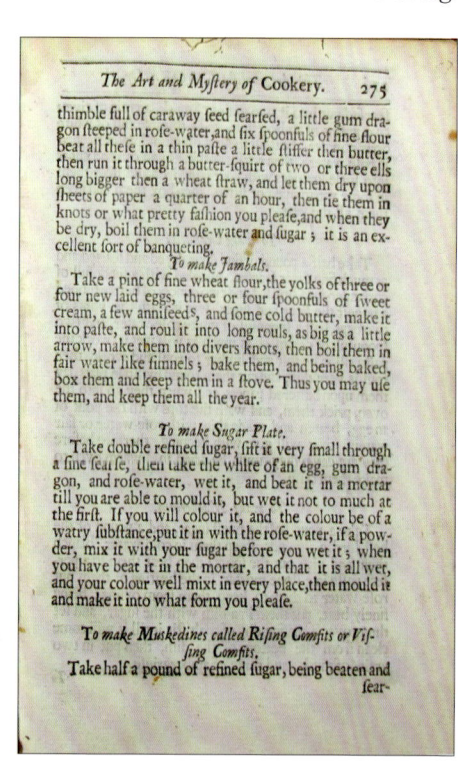

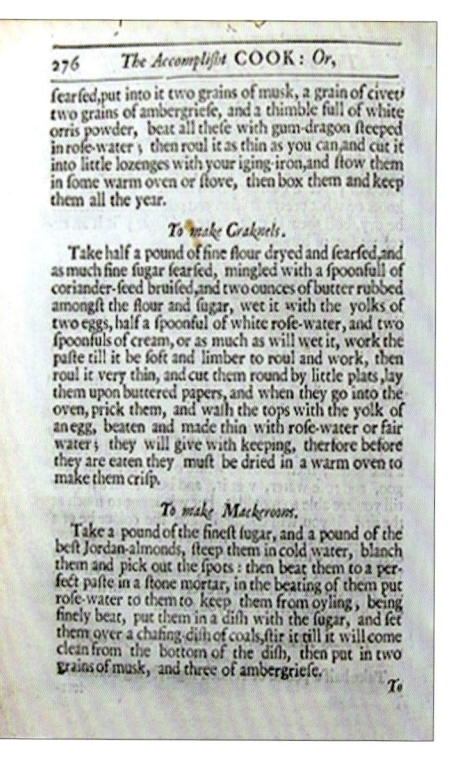

306 Robert May's recipe for "Muskedines called Rising Comfits or Vissing Comfits", the latter no doubt a misprint for "Kissing Comfits".
Note the use of the term "iging-iron" for the more usual "jigging iron", either a very rare usage or perhaps another misprint.

Photograph the author, courtesy Ivan Day

Pastry Jiggers and Pastry Prints

307 Muscadines or Kissing Comfits made to Robert May's recipe by Ivan Day.
Photograph courtesy Ivan Day

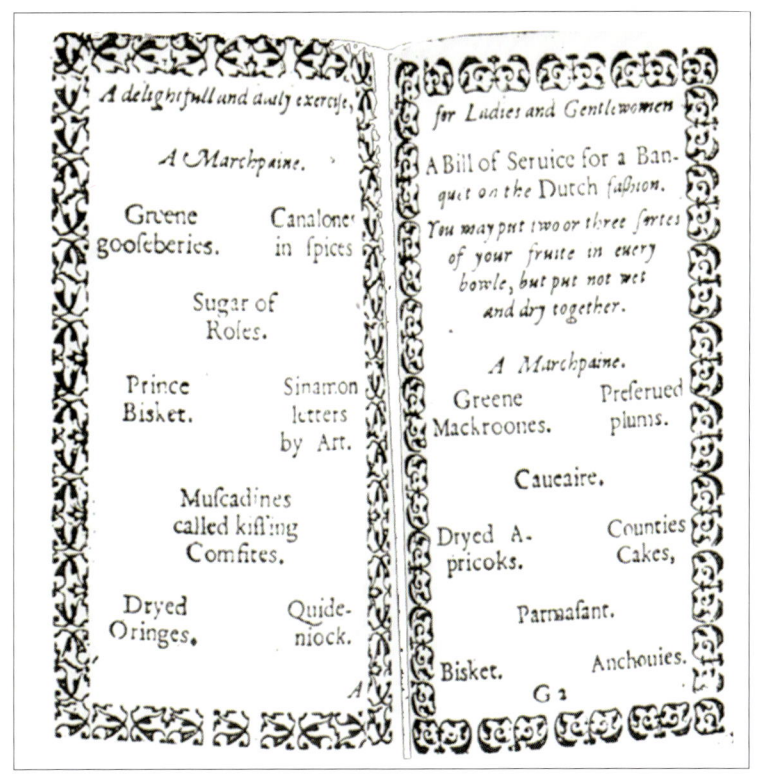

308 John Murell's "Bill of Service for a Banquet on the Dutch fashion" including "Muscadines called kissing Comfites", from his *A Delightfull and Daily Exercise for Ladies and Gentlewomen*, published in London, 1621.

Courtesy Ivan Day

Pastry Jiggers and Pastry Prints

310 A minced beef lattice-topped pie made by the author using this Italian two-wheeled jigger; the rim is impressed with its rosette print at intervals.

309 An Italian late 16th-/early 17th-century bronze jigger. 180mm.

MF 033

Pastry Jiggers and Pastry Prints

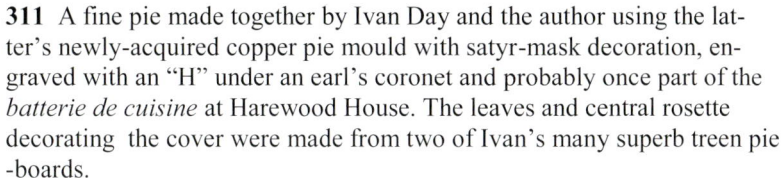

311 A fine pie made together by Ivan Day and the author using the latter's newly-acquired copper pie mould with satyr-mask decoration, engraved with an "H" under an earl's coronet and probably once part of the *batterie de cuisine* at Harewood House. The leaves and central rosette decorating the cover were made from two of Ivan's many superb treen pie-boards.

The wavy edge, known as a "crinkum-crankum", was very simply made by a series of impressions of the arc of the jigger (right) used flat, each pair of impressions interspersed with an upward nudge of Ivan's index finger.

The mould now has pride of place in Ivan's fine collection of early pie moulds. For an entertaining account of its checkered history, once converted to a jardinière, its restoration to its original use and the making of this pie, see Ivan's *Food History Jottings* for 22nd December, 2012, at www.historicfood.com

Photograph the author, courtesy Ivan Day

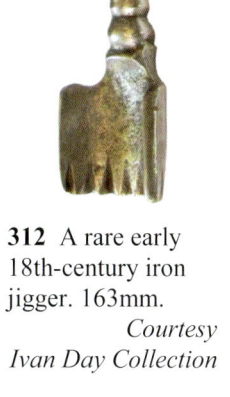

312 A rare early 18th-century iron jigger. 163mm.
Courtesy Ivan Day Collection

313, 314 Carved wooden pie-boards from which were moulded the central rosette and the leaves on the lid of the pie above. 118mm and 155mm long.
Courtesy Ivan Day Collection

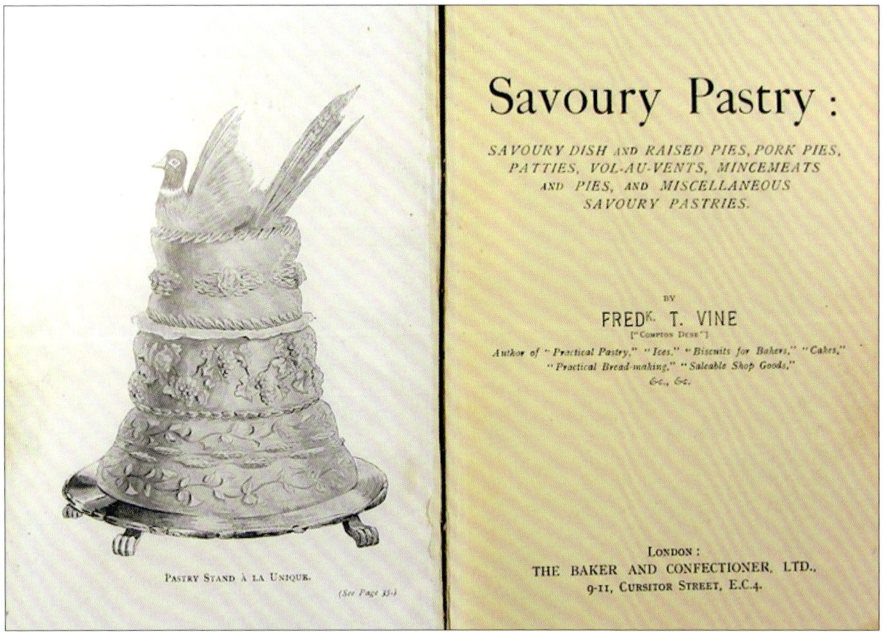

Pastry Jiggers and Pastry Prints

In addition to their prime purpose, recipe books may also be useful in showing contemporary kitchen equipment or that in use in the fairly recent past. Frederick T. Vine's *Savoury Pastry*, published in London, must date from after 1917 when the district numbering system including E.C. 4, which appears on its title page, was introduced. Nonetheless, it depicts a jigger with leaf-shaped cutter dating from the late 19th century, a Victorian pastry nipper or crimper and a Victorian heavy-duty jigger referred to as a "crinkled Paste Wheel". As will be seen from the example illustrated below, such pastry wheels were made by Messrs. Benham and Froud, probably in the mid 19th century. It should be noted, however, that the firm was in business until 1922.

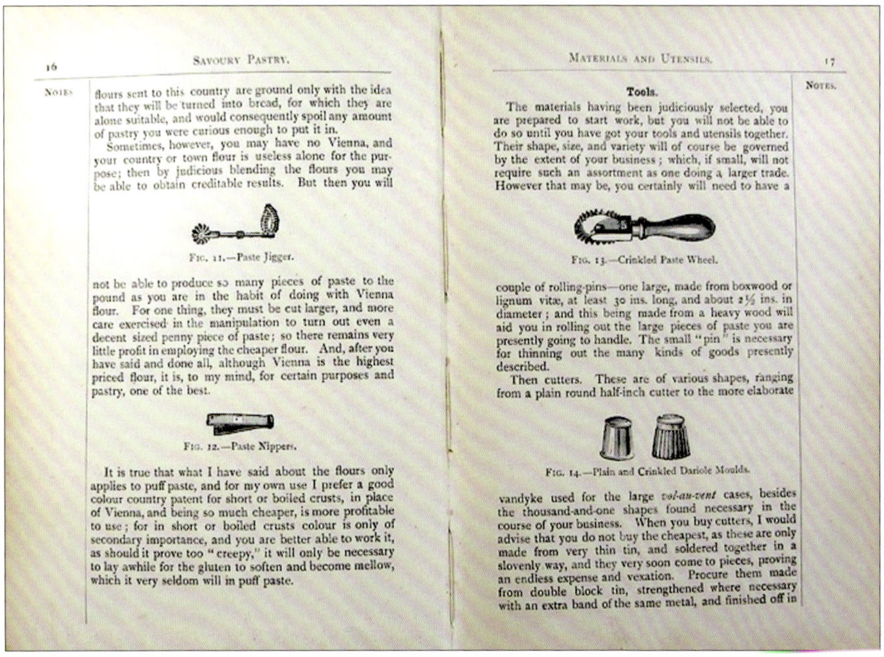

315, 316 From *Savoury Pastry* by Frederick T. Vine, London early 20th Century.
Courtesy Ivan Day Collection

317 A brass jigger with leaf-shaped cutter, very similar to that illustrated above. 110mm.
Private Collection

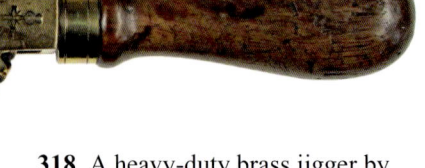

318 A heavy-duty brass jigger by Benham & Froud, very similar to that illustrated above, about 110mm.
MF 108

319 A brass "paste nipper" or crimper. 104mm.
MF 206

Pastry Jiggers and Pastry Prints

PASTRY SAMPLES
made using the jiggers and prints in
the author's collection.

To refer to the implement which made each sample, please see page 74, where the collection numbers are correlated with the relevant page numbers.

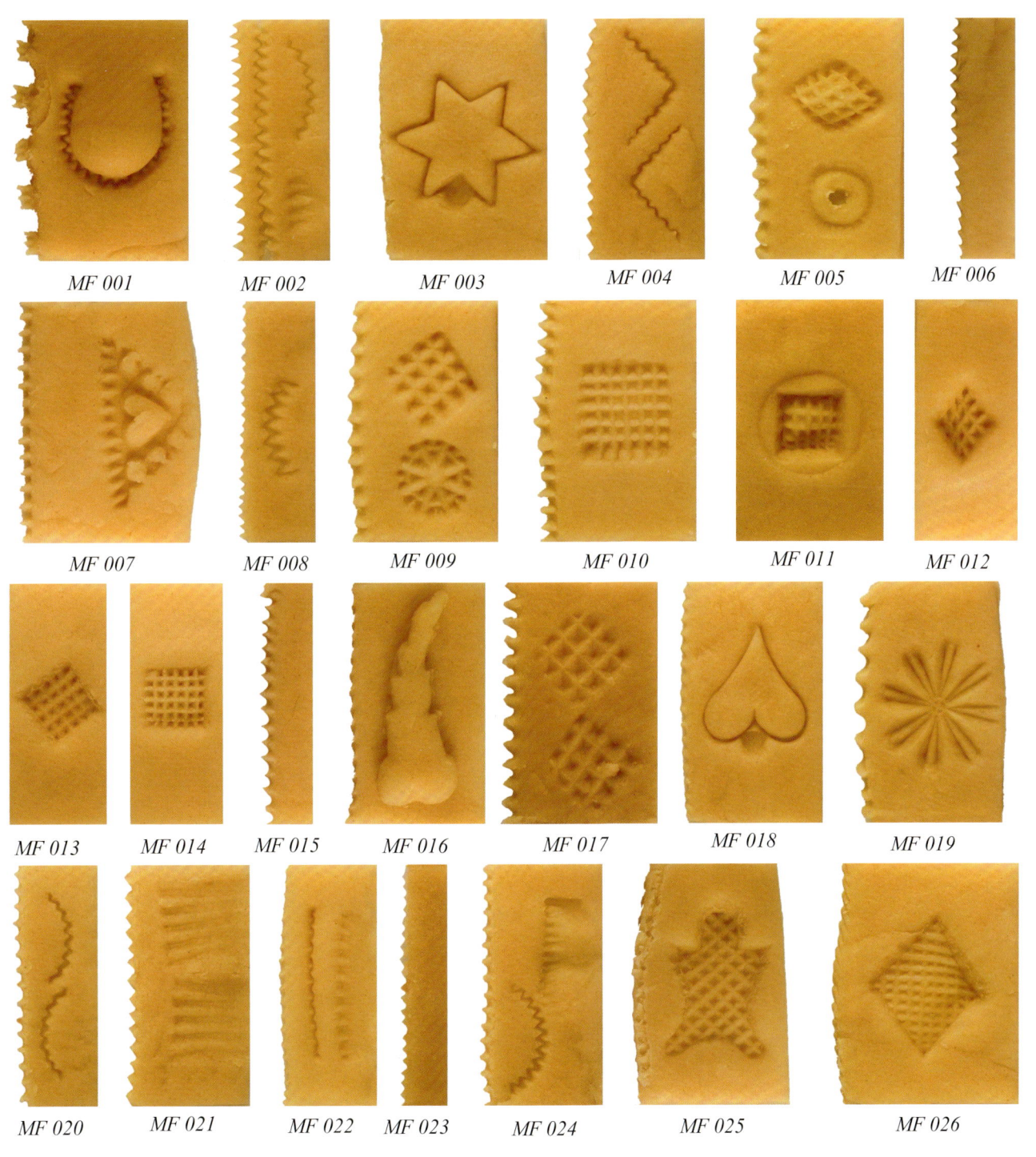

MF 001	MF 002	MF 003	MF 004	MF 005	MF 006
MF 007	MF 008	MF 009	MF 010	MF 011	MF 012
MF 013	MF 014	MF 015	MF 016	MF 017	MF 018	MF 019
MF 020	MF 021	MF 022	MF 023	MF 024	MF 025	MF 026

Pastry Jiggers and Pastry Prints

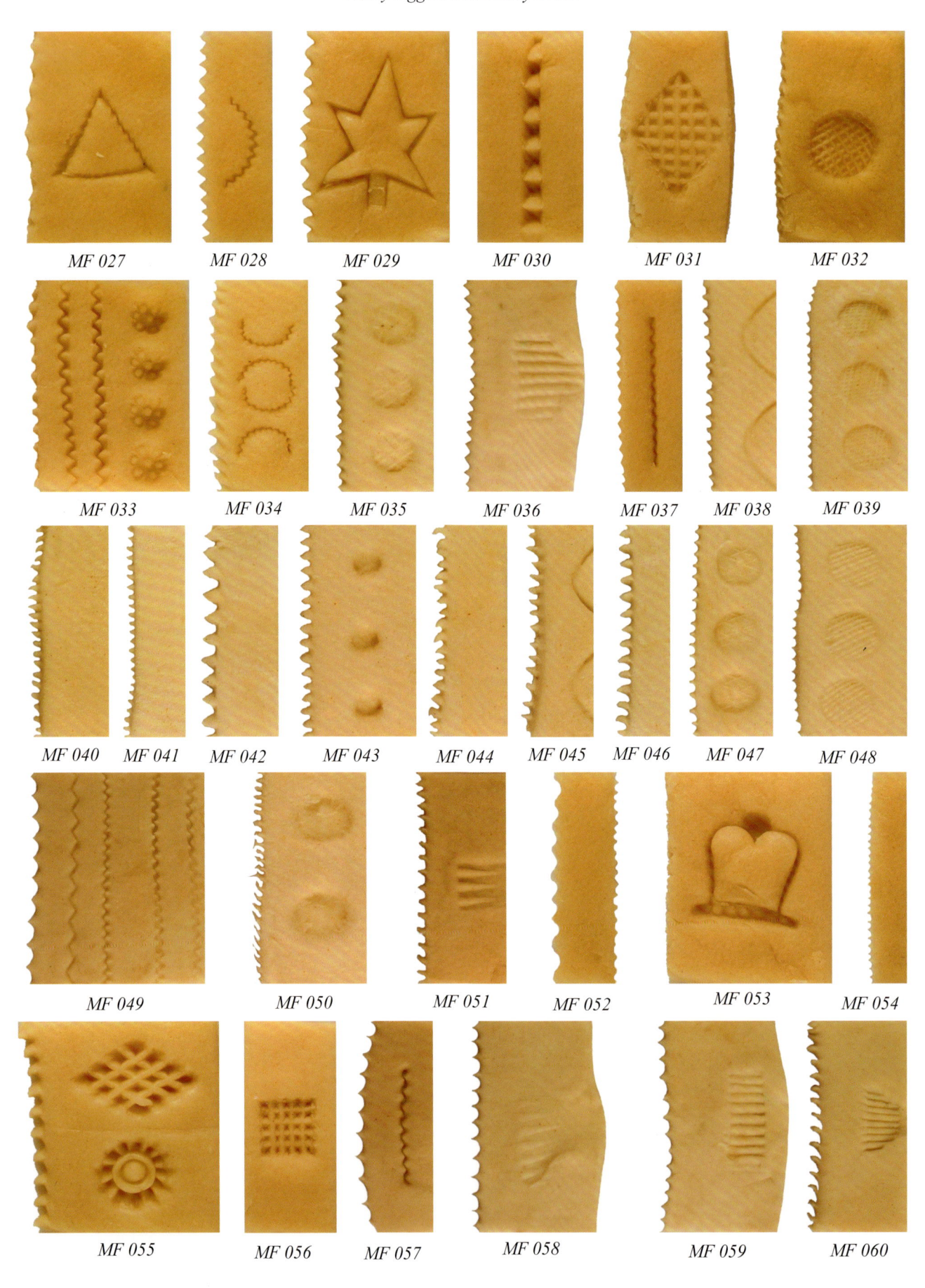

MF 027	MF 028	MF 029	MF 030	MF 031	MF 032
MF 033	MF 034	MF 035	MF 036	MF 037	MF 038	MF 039
MF 040	MF 041	MF 042	MF 043	MF 044	MF 045	MF 046	MF 047	MF 048
MF 049	MF 050	MF 051	MF 052	MF 053	MF 054
MF 055	MF 056	MF 057	MF 058	MF 059	MF 060

Pastry Jiggers and Pastry Prints

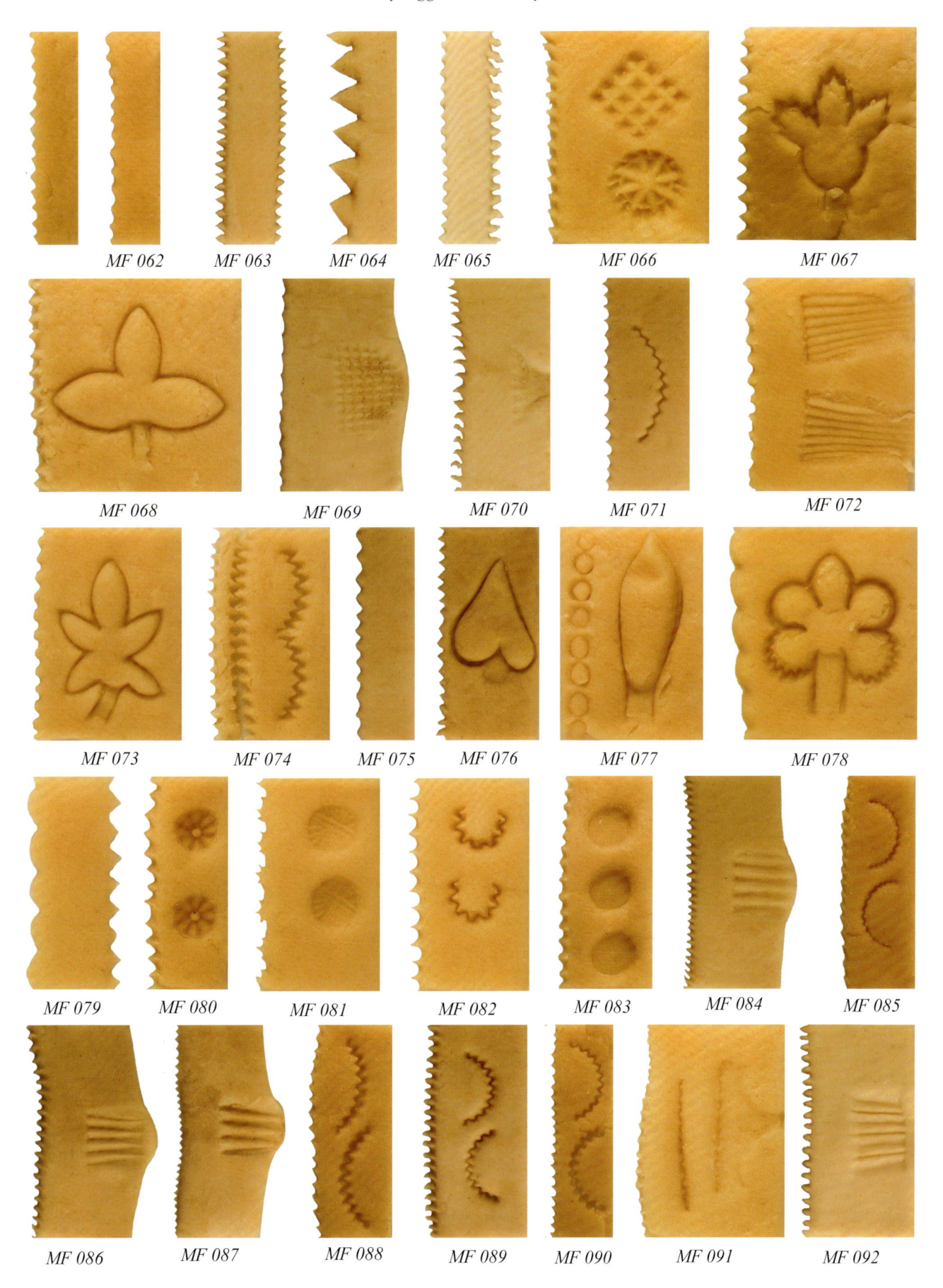

MF 062 MF 063 MF 064 MF 065 MF 066 MF 067

MF 068 MF 069 MF 070 MF 071 MF 072

MF 073 MF 074 MF 075 MF 076 MF 077 MF 078

MF 079 MF 080 MF 081 MF 082 MF 083 MF 084 MF 085

MF 086 MF 087 MF 088 MF 089 MF 090 MF 091 MF 092

Pastry Jiggers and Pastry Prints

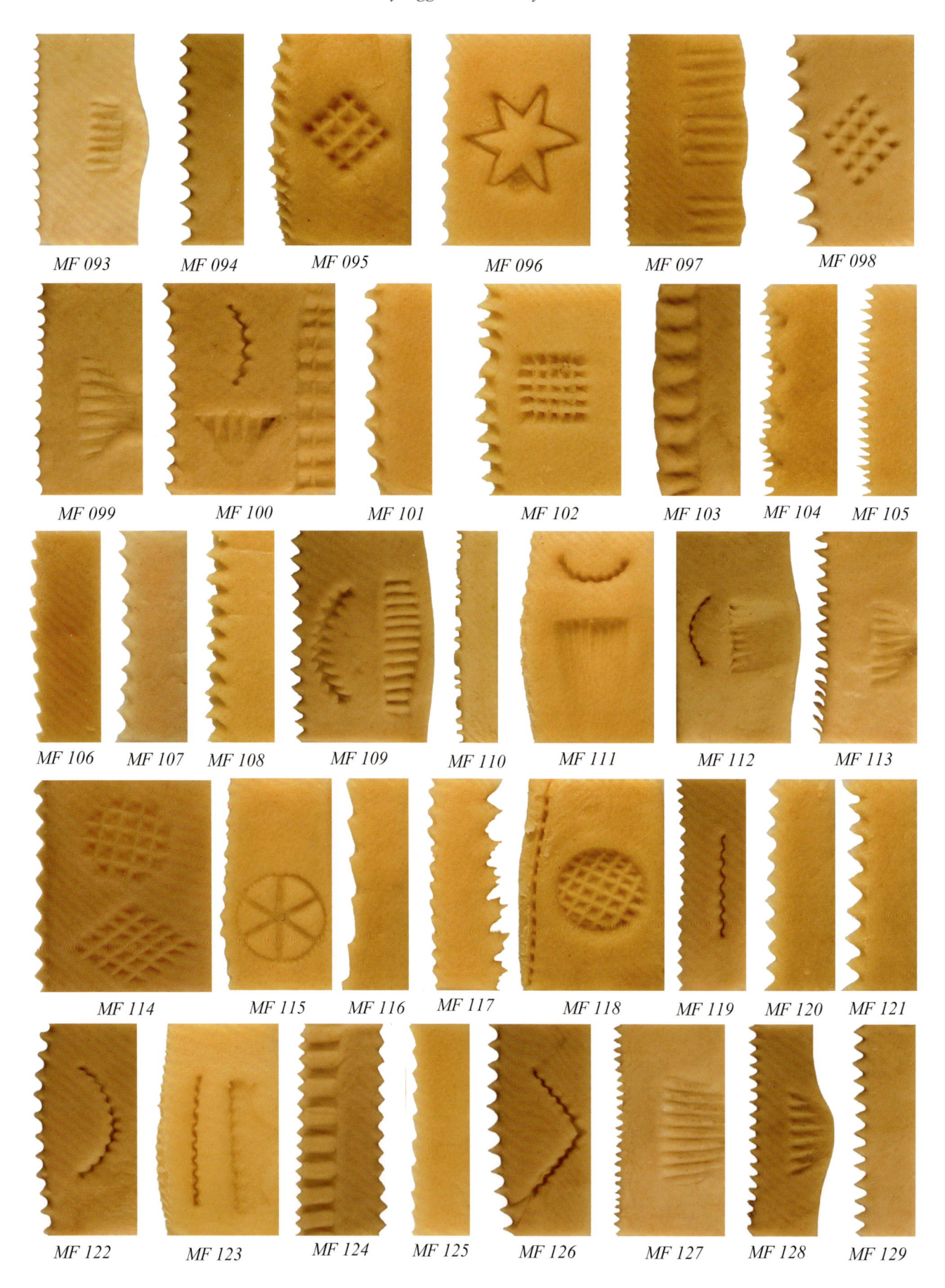

MF 093	MF 094	MF 095	MF 096	MF 097	MF 098
MF 099	MF 100	MF 101	MF 102	MF 103	MF 104 · MF 105
MF 106 · MF 107 · MF 108	MF 109	MF 110 · MF 111	MF 112	MF 113	
MF 114	MF 115 · MF 116	MF 117	MF 118	MF 119	MF 120 · MF 121
MF 122	MF 123	MF 124 · MF 125	MF 126	MF 127	MF 128 · MF 129

Pastry Jiggers and Pastry Prints

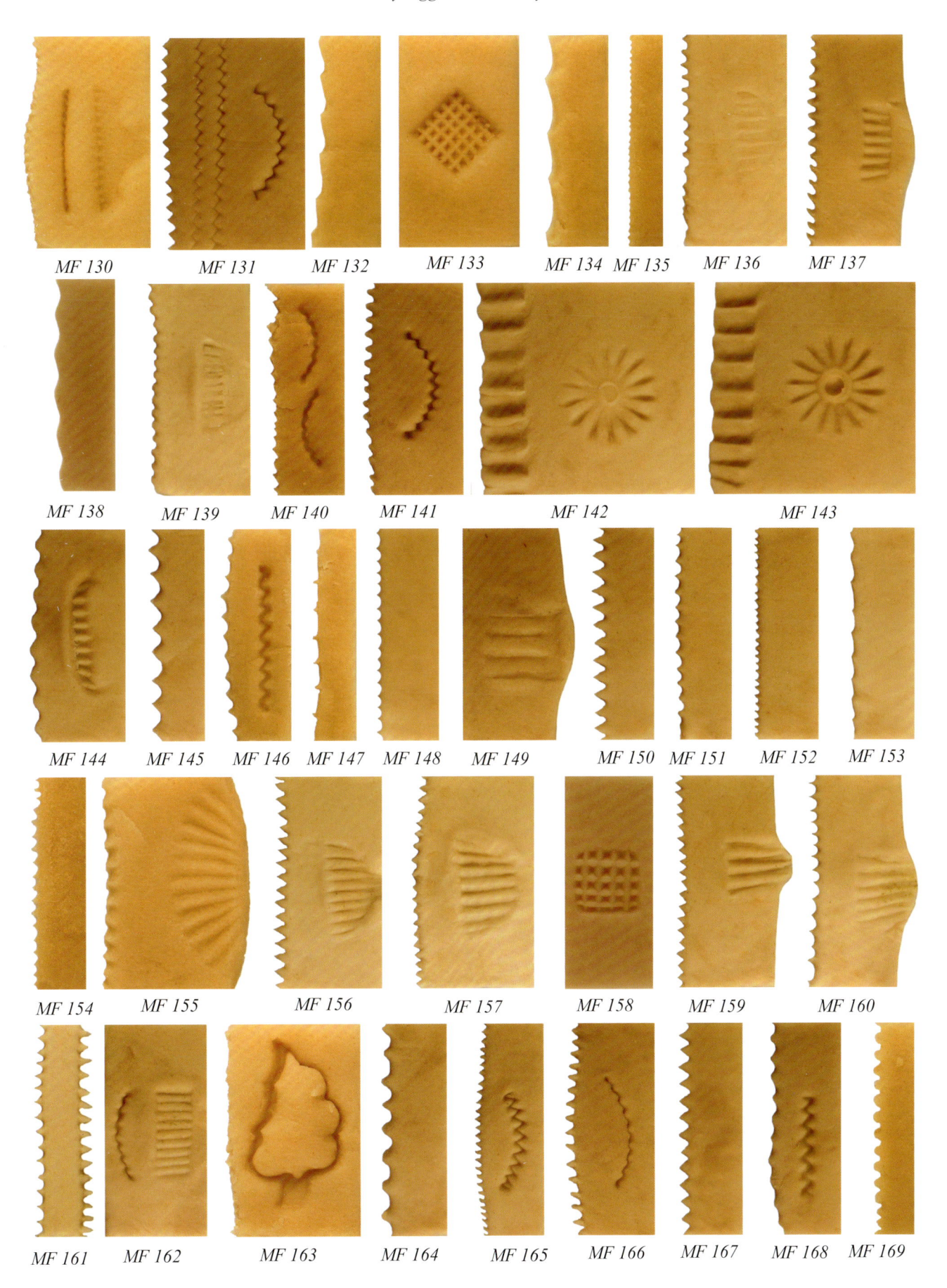

| MF 130 | MF 131 | MF 132 | MF 133 | MF 134 | MF 135 | MF 136 | MF 137 |

| MF 138 | MF 139 | MF 140 | MF 141 | MF 142 | MF 143 |

| MF 144 | MF 145 | MF 146 | MF 147 | MF 148 | MF 149 | MF 150 | MF 151 | MF 152 | MF 153 |

| MF 154 | MF 155 | MF 156 | MF 157 | MF 158 | MF 159 | MF 160 |

| MF 161 | MF 162 | MF 163 | MF 164 | MF 165 | MF 166 | MF 167 | MF 168 | MF 169 |

Pastry Jiggers and Pastry Prints

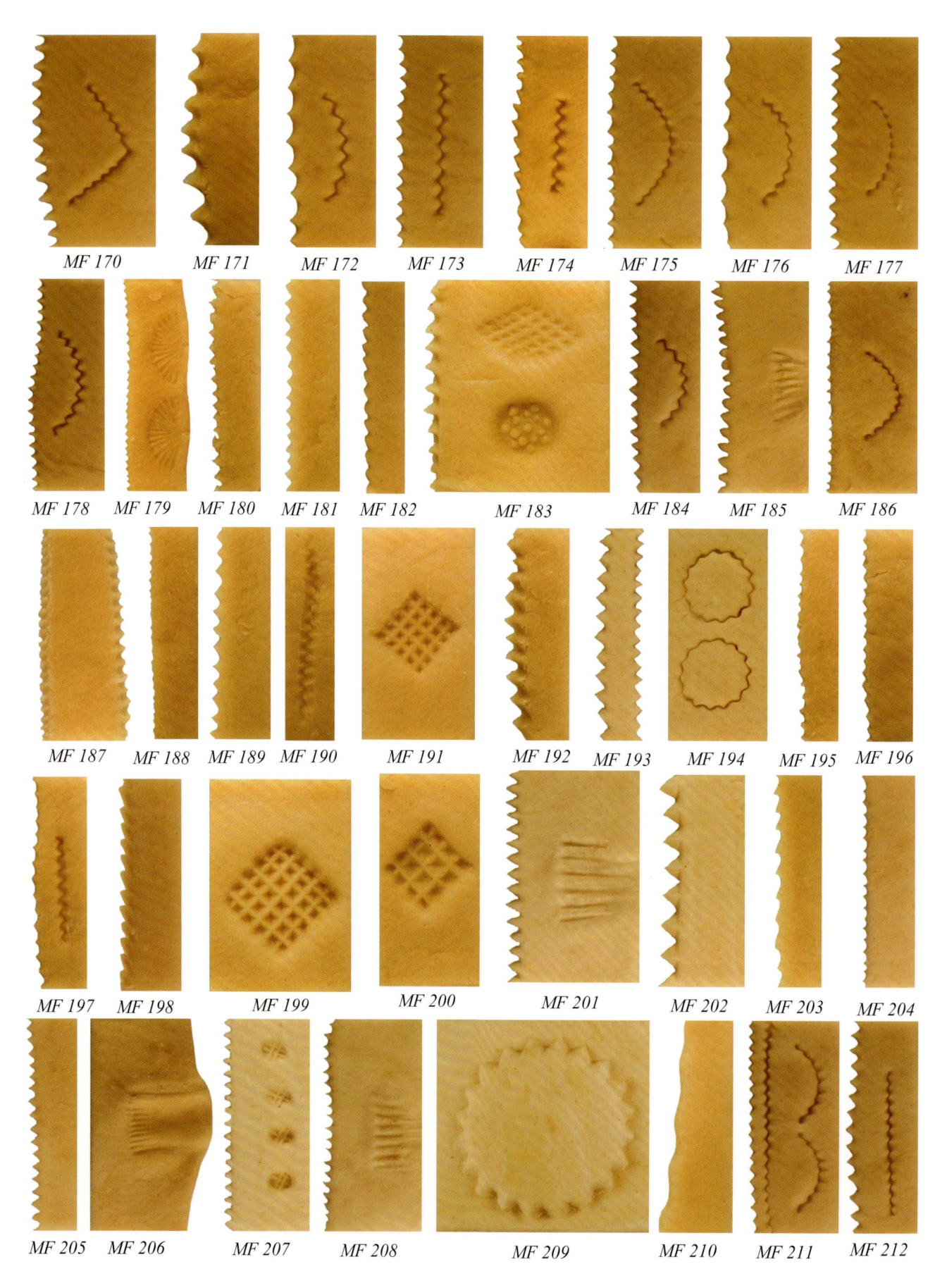

MF 170	MF 171	MF 172	MF 173	MF 174	MF 175	MF 176	MF 177
MF 178	MF 179	MF 180	MF 181	MF 182	MF 183	MF 184	MF 185	MF 186
MF 187	MF 188	MF 189	MF 190	MF 191	MF 192	MF 193	MF 194	MF 195	MF 196
MF 197	MF 198	MF 199	MF 200	MF 201	MF 202	MF 203	MF 204
MF 205	MF 206	MF 207	MF 208	MF 209	MF 210	MF 211	MF 212

Pastry Jiggers and Pastry Prints

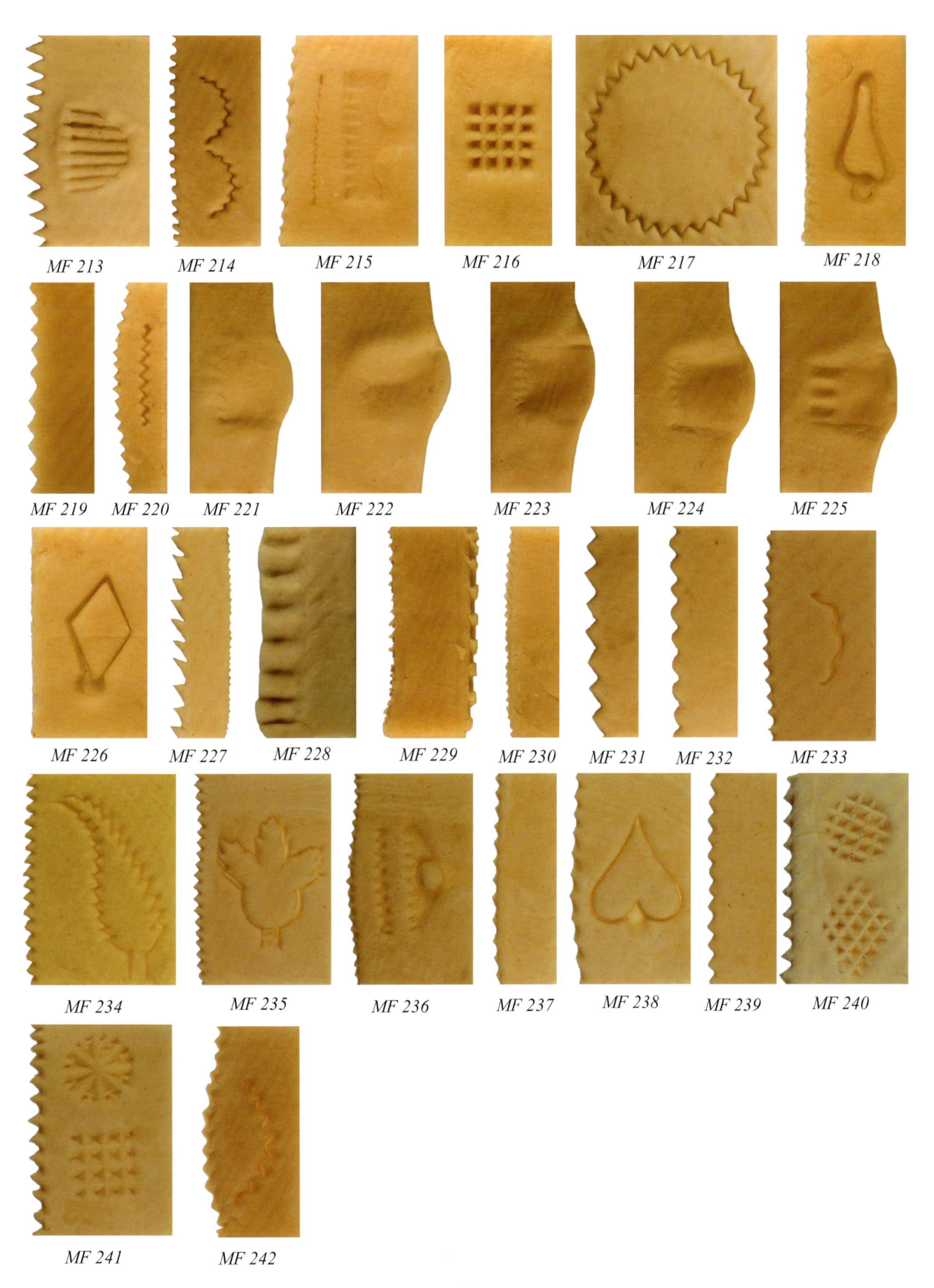

MF 213	MF 214	MF 215	MF 216	MF 217	MF 218
MF 219	MF 220	MF 221	MF 222	MF 223	MF 224	MF 225
MF 226	MF 227	MF 228	MF 229	MF 230	MF 231	MF 232	MF 233
MF 234	MF 235	MF 236	MF 237	MF 238	MF 239	MF 240
MF 241	MF 242

Correlation Michael Finlay Collection Numbers and Pages

MF No.	Page	MF No.	Page	MF No.	Page	MF No.	Page	MF No.	Page	MF No.	Page	MF No.	Page
001	12	038	54	075	44	112	12	149	11	186	22	223	5
002	27	039	55	076	26	113	32	150	52	187	25	224	5
003	26	040	54	077	29	114	60	151	43	188	17	225	5
004	26	041	55	078	24	115	29	152	43	189	47	226	29
005	34	042	55	079	24	116	45	153	43	190	17	227	49
006	44	043	55	080	12	117	13	154	18	191	38	228	53
007	12	044	54	081	12	118	39	155	43	192	24	229	25
008	22	045	54	082	24	119	22	156	32	193	49	230	9
009	35	046	55	083	12	120	47	157	31	194	48	231	44
010	34	047	54	084	30	121	47	158	38	195	22	232	44
011	39	048	55	085	42	122	23	159	30	196	47	233	24
012	38	049	75	086	30	123	18	160	30	197	49	234	28
013	38	050	54	087	30	124	51	161	25	198	42	235	28
014	38	051	30	088	24	125	47	162	27	199	38	236	49
015	9	052	25	089	24	126	22	163	26	200	39	237	42
016	29	053	28	090	24	127	32	164	51	201	32	238	28
017	39	054	17	091	18	128	31	165	22	202	57	239	25
018	29	055	34	092	31	129	44	166	27	203	48	240	36
019	29	056	38	093	32	130	18	167	51	204	48	241	37
020	23	057	23	094	44	131	22	168	51	205	48	242	51
021	30	058	31	095	39	132	45	169	47	206	11		
022	18	059	27	096	28	133	39	170	22	207	55		
023	17	060	31	097	30	134	45	171	40	208	32		
024	22	061	46	098	38	135	11	172	51	209	48		
025	29	062	25	099	31	136	32	173	22	210	45		
026	39	063	26	100	50	137	32	174	23	211	22		
027	28	064	21	101	46	138	53	175	23	212	23		
028	24	065	25	102	35	139	26	176	23	213	31		
029	28	066	35	103	53	140	42	177	23	214	23		
030	15	067	28	104	43	141	22	178	23	215	18		
031	26	068	28	105	12	142	52	179	19	216	38		
032	39	069	32	106	46	143	52	180	9	217	48		
033	11	070	31	107	45	144	52	181	58	218	29		
034	12	071	23	108	46	145	51	182	44	219	48		
035	54	072	31	109	44	146	49	183	37	220	49		
036	32	073	28	110	12	147	42	184	22	221	5		
037	19	074	22	111	12	148	43	185	32	222	5		

SCRIMSHAW PASTRY JIGGERS

320 A mid to late 20th-century bone scrimshaw jigger following an old tradition, the heart-piercings suggesting its making as a love token. It is believed such artefacts are also made for competition purposes. 210mm long.

MF 049

The pastry jiggers so far considered in this work have been largely craftsman-made wood and metal kitchen implements intended for everyday use in the kitchen. There is, however an entirely different class of jiggers, those elevated to an art form known as "scrimshaw", certainly a folk art. These were the work of whalers, mainly in the nineteenth century, during the slack times of their long voyages in search of their quarry, or perhaps during the intervals between their voyages. Not only pastry jiggers but a wide range of other artefacts were the result of the work of these whalers who became known as "scrimshanders", and who, often with great skill and artistry, used the by-products of their industry to create these works of art.

The main purpose of the whalers was to find and kill whales, mainly the two species known as right whales and sperm whales, which have a thick layer of fat, known as blubber, to be rendered down at sea into whale oil, useful for many purposes but particularly as a lamp oil for domestic lighting. The by-products of this work included white whalebone, the skeletal structure of the animal, particularly the pan-bone, part of the lower jaw. They also used baleen, a dark bony mouth-part material, in plates which formed the screen, often as much as four metres in height, through which the whale strained the plankton which was its main source of food, and whale ivory, from the whales' teeth. Walrus ivory, from the tusks of that animal, was also prized.

Whalers, on voyages which could last several years and reach far-flung seas, also used other exotic materials for decoration, such as abalone shell, mother-of pearl and tortoiseshell, (actually usually from the shell or carapace of the Hawksbill turtle).

Among the many things produced were decorated whales' teeth, engraved with a needle-like point, often demonstrating immense skill, with commemorative scenes or figures; vessels and whaling scenes were also popular subjects. Lamp black, mixed with oil, was then rubbed into the scratch-engraved decoration, giving it permanence. Such decorated teeth are now keenly sought after and command high prices, as do most types of scrimshaw work.

Whalebone was also used to create the tools used by the sailors themselves, such as fids to open the weave of ropes for splicing, seam rubbers for sail-making, pulley blocks and the like. It was also used to fashion almost anything in the way of small domestic artefacts otherwise made in wood. Many of these whalebone artefacts were made as presents for wives and girlfriends and incorporated hearts as love tokens. The same applied to articles made in baleen such as stay busks, often personalised with names and verses.

As will be seen from the ensuing illustrations, scrimshaw pastry jiggers were produced with great skill and care, but it is probable that many were made purely as love tokens and not intended for everyday use as pastry wheels. Because of this likelihood, and the large sums which good examples command, often running into thousand of pounds sterling, the present author has chosen not to include such jiggers in his collection, with the exception of that above, but for completeness's sake here includes a selection of typical museum specimens.

For further reading please see the Bibliography.

Pastry Jiggers and Pastry Prints

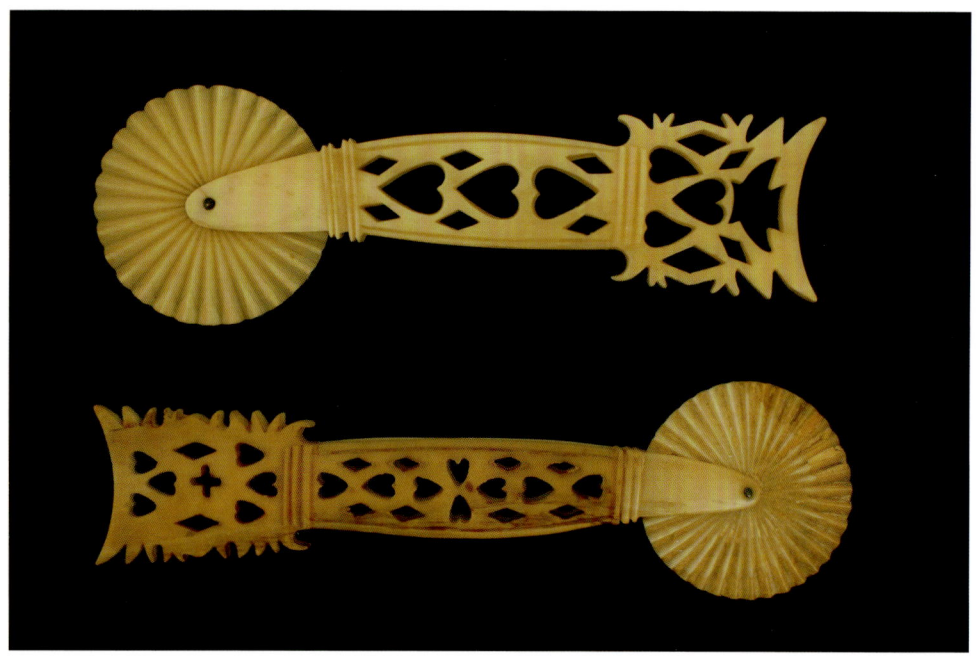

321 Two fine examples of the whaler's art in whale ivory, the upper one carved from a single sperm whale tooth by Captain John Marble of the barque *Kathleen* of New Bedford, 1857-60. 156mm long. *Ref: 2001.100.1837.*

The lower example is also of whale ivory. 162mm long. *Ref: 2009.47.3.*

Courtesy of the New Bedford Whaling Museum

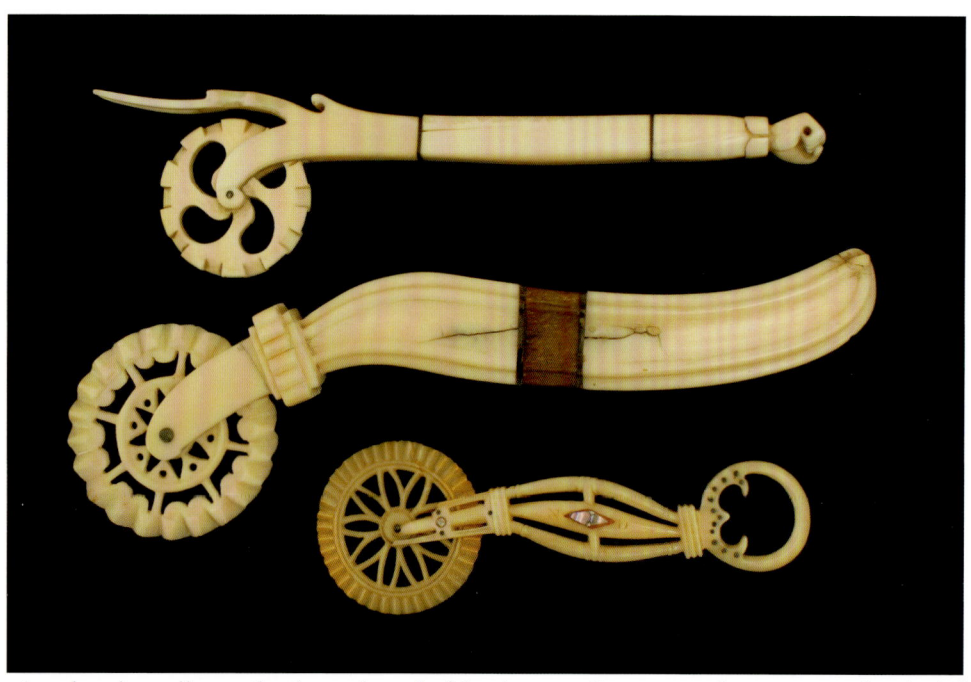

322 A walrus-ivory jigger, the three-piece shaft having non-ferrous metal separators, clenched-fist terminal pierced for a suspension ring, and two-tined fork, the pierced wheel with crenellated edge. 200mm long. *Ref: 00.146.12.*

A whale-ivory jigger, the handle having a central wooden section between two thin bands of baleen, reed-carved chamfered edges, the wheel intricately pierced. 221mm long. *Ref: 2001.100.790.*

A walrus-ivory jigger with ring terminal, pierced shaft inlaid with abalone shell and with red wax, engraved initials, "N.D." and extremely finely-pierced nine-petal openwork wheel. 134mm long. *Ref: 2001.100.709.*

Courtesy of the New Bedford Whaling Museum

Pastry Jiggers and Pastry Prints

323 A very elegantly carved whale-ivory jigger in the form of a mythical beast, a hippocampus, Neptune's steed, with unicorn's head, a three-tined fork in lieu of its single horn, the body with a central band of ebony, its fluke forming a ring for suspension, with a star-pierced wheel. 197mm long. *Ref: 1923.7.2.*

Another similar jigger with baleen trim, three-tined fork and fluted wheel. 243mm long. *Ref: 2001.100.569.*

Courtesy of the New Bedford Whaling Museum

324 A whale-ivory jigger the shaft divided by three bands of wood with silver-metal separators and terminating in a three-tine fork. 240mm long. *Ref: 1923.7.55.*

A whale-ivory jigger with loop handle for suspension, four-tined fork and star-pierced wheel finished on one side only. 204mm long. *Ref: 1923.7.89.*

A whale-bone and whale-ivory jigger, the panbone shaft having pierced openwork sections each of four columns, the carved ball finial and finely pierced wheel of whale ivory. 254mm long. *Ref: 1923.7.82.*

A whale-ivory open work jigger of geometric construction, with double-pierced wheel. 216mm long. *Ref: 1923.7.6.*

Courtesy of the New Bedford Whaling Museum

Pastry Jiggers and Pastry Prints

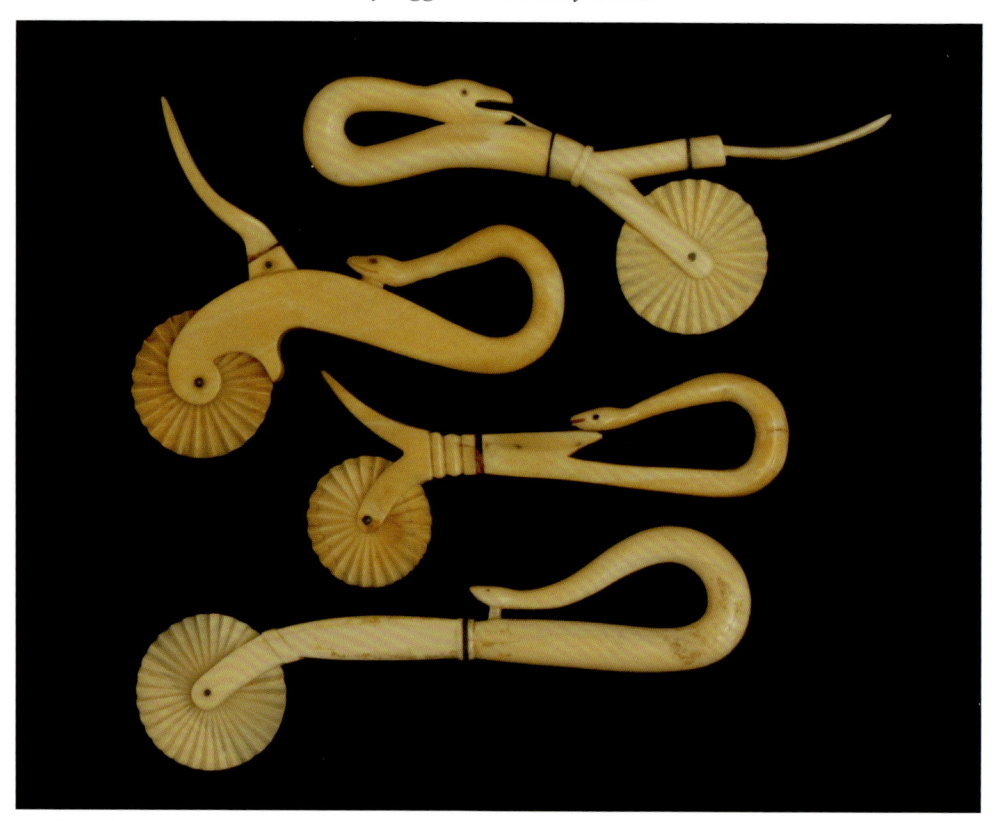

325 Four literally serpentine jiggers:

A walrus-ivory example, the serpent's mouth open with visible tongue, its neck forming a loop for suspension, the sections with baleen dividers, with three-tined fork and fluted wheel. 187mm long. *Ref: 2001.100.552.*

Another, walrus ivory, its eyes inlaid with red wax, the body flattening to form the wheel supports, also with three-tined fork and fluted wheel. 138mm long. *Ref: 2001.100.879.*

A whale-ivory example, the two-sectional body with red wax divider, the mouth similarly reddened, with three-tined fork. 153mm long. *Ref: 1923.7.11.*

Another, whale ivory, the serpentine handle in two sections with tortoiseshell divider. 196mm long. *Ref: 1923.7.83.*

Courtesy of the New Bedford Whaling Museum

BIBLIOGRAPHY

MAGAZINE AND JOURNAL ARTICLES

Haze, Wellington, *Jagging Wheels,* Antiques, Volume I, June, 1922, pp. 260-262.

Lantz, Louise, K., *Pie Crimpers and Pastry Jaggers,* Spinning Wheel, October, 1966, p. 22.

BOOKS

D'Allemagne, Henry René, *Decorative Antique Ironwork, A Pictorial Treasury,* Dover Publications, Inc., New York,1968, p. 354.
SBN 486 22082 6.

Borella, Mr., *The Court and Country Confectioner,* London, 1772.

Bradley, Richard, *The Country Housewife and Lady's Director,* London, 1736.

Franklin, Linda Campbell, 300 Years of Kitchen Collectibles, 5th Edition, Krause Publications, 2003. Includes a useful section covering many later US patents for jiggers.
ISBN 0 87349 365 6.

Garrett, Theodore Francis, (Ed.), *Encyclopædia of Practical Cookery,* London, 1892.

Gentle, Rupert and Field, Rachel, revised by Gentle, Belinda, *Domestic Metalwork, 1640-1820,* Antique Collectors' Club, Woodbridge, 1994, pp. 239-240. Illustrates a number of jiggers.
ISBN 1 85149 187 2.

Goufé, Jules, *The Royal Book of Pastry and Confectionery,* London, 1874.

Lawrence, Martha, *Scrimshaw The Whaler's Legacy,* Schiffer Publications, 1983, a general treatise on the art of the whaler which has a well-illustrated coverage of scrimshaw jiggers, pp. 94-99.
ISBN 0 88740 455 3.

Lecoq, Raymond, *Les Objets de la vie domestique,* Berger-Levrault, Paris, pp. 259-260. Illustrates a few examples.
ISBN 13 9782701302188.

Lindsay, J. Seymour, *Iron and Brass Implements of the English House,* Alec Tiranti, London, 1970. Illustrates a few examples.
ISBN 0 85458 999 6.

May, Robert, *The Accomplisht Cook, or the Art and Mystery of Cooking,* London, 1685.

McManus, Michael, *A Treasury of American Scrimshaw,* Penguin Studio, 1997, a general treatise on scrimshaw with only a handful of jiggers illustrated, pp. 58 and 60.
ISBN 0 670 86234 7.

Murell, John, *A Delightful and Daily Exercise for Ladies and Gentlewomen,* London, 1621.

Pinto, Edward, H., *Treen and other wooden bygones,* Bell, London, 1969. Only a brief mention, illustrating three examples.
ISBN 0 7135 1533 3.

Plummer, Don, *Colonial Wrought Iron, the Sorber Collection,* Skipjack Press, Ocean Pines, Maryland, 1999, pp.74-75.
ISBN 13 9781879535169.

Scappi, Bartolomeo, *Opera,* Venice, 1570. Facsimile reprint, Lightning Source, U.K. Ltd., Milton Keynes.
ISBN 9 781174 933 41 7.

Varenne, François Pierre La, *Le Pâtissier François,* Paris 1653. Another edition, Elzevier Press, Amsterdam, 1655.

Vine, Frederick, T., *Savoury Pastry,* London, c.1920.

CATALOGUES

Cartland, James and Sons. Catalogue of small metalwares including jiggers, Birmingham, 1894.

H.H.E. probably for Huxley, the name written boldly on the fore-edge. Catalogue of small metalwares including several jiggers, late 19th century.

Morehouse Wells, Catalogue of hardware, etc., including a few jiggers, Decatur, Illinois, 1894.

Walker, Philip, (Ed.), *The Victorian Catalogue of Tools for Trades and Crafts,* circa 1845. Facsimile reprint, No date, late 20th century. Illustrates four examples as "Paste Markers Brass or Iron".
ISBN 1 85891 120 6.

INDEX

Auctioneers:
   Christies' South Kensington, 18
   Dukes, Dorchester, 19
   Koller Auctions, Zurich, 11
   Smith, Andrew & Sons, Itchen Stoke, 41
   Sotheby's, London, 18

Companies:
   Benham and Froud, 46, 66
   Cartland, James and Sons, 27
   Chiarugi Brothers, 51
   East, George (Housewares) Ltd., 53
   H.H.E., probably Huxley, 26, 27, 28
   Lechner and Stump, 50
   Morehouse [and] Wells, 23
   Nutbrown, 53
   Stephenson Mills, 53
   Taylor-Law & Co, (Tala), 53

Collections:
   Albert Collection, 19
   Butler, Roderick, 16, 17, 26, 27
   Croft-Lyons Bequest, 11
   Davis, Carl J, 40, 41, 42
   Day, Ivan, 3, 13, 21, 29, 48, 57, 58, 62, 63, 65, 66
   Michael Finlay, 2-5, 9, 11-13, 15-19, 21-32, 34-40, 42-61, 64, 66
   Gant, Julia, 37
   Hahn, Gary, 40
   Harrison, Edward, 16, 39
   Navarro, A.F. de, 16
   Nessi Collection, 11
   Rabaiotti, Renato, 9, 13, 49
   Seeger, Stanley, J., 18, 19
   Walker, James, 18, 19

Dealers:
   Dickenson, Alastair, London, 18
   Holt, Carole, 40, 41
   Stone, Eve, Antiques, 33

Jiggers, Pastry prints:
   Alternative names for -
     Coggling wheels, 2
     Coq de pâtissier, 9
     Cookie and Pastry Tool, 52
     Crimpers, 5, 50, 52
     Dough knives, 5, 13
     Dough cutters, 2
     Dough spurs, 2
     Fancy markers, 4, 27
     Gigling irons, 2
     Iging-iron, 62
     Jagger, 2
     Jagging-Irons, 1
     Jagging wheels, 2
     Jigger, 2
     Molete per pasta, 2, 5, 10, 11, 52
     Paste nipper, 66
     Paste-prints, 1, 4,
     Pastry cutter, 50
     Pie rimmer, 50
     Pie crimper, 52
     Pie sealer, 2
     Pie trimmer, 2
     Roulettes de pâtissier , 24
     Sperone da pasticiero, 1, 8, 9, 12
     Sperone da pasta, 1, 10,

Libraries:
   Bibliotèque Nationale, Paris, 14
   Pepys Library, Magdalene College, Cambridge, 20

Miscellanea:
   Pastry samples, 67
   Whalers, whaling, 75
     Barque "Kathleen", 76
     Baleen, 75
     Scrimshaw, 75
     Walrus ivory, 75
     Whalebone, 75
     Whale's teeth, 65

Museums:
   British Museum, 9, 11
   Gloucester Folk Museum, 17
   Fitzwilliam Museum, Cambridge, 16
   New Bedford Whaling Museum, 77-78
   V. & A. Museum, 9, 11, 13
   York Castle Museum, 19

People:
Bacon, Sir Francis, 3
Bingham, Abel, 1
Bingham, Thomas, 1, 4,
Butler, Robin, 19
Carr, William, M.A., 3
Eeckhout, Gerbrand van den, 15
Hakewill, James, 20
Kepp, John, Edward and Richard, 46
La Varenne, 14
Leqoc, Raymond, 24

Pepys, Samuel, 20
Pereda, Antonio, 21
Pius V, Pope, 1
Marble, Captain John, 76
May, Robert, 21
Meystnor, Nathaniel, 19, 20
Reynard, Mr., 57
Scappi, Bartolomeo, 1, 5, 7, 8, 9, 10, 11, 12, 52
Woodforde, Parson, 57

Places:
United States of America, 46
   Illinois, 23
     Chicago, 51, 52
     Decatur, 23
   Pennsylvania, 24, 25, 43
     Sheridan, 50
   Minnesota, 51
     Minneapolis, 51
Austria, 45
   Vienna, 45
Baltic, 49
Britain, 25, 51
Canada, 25
China, 52
Czechoslovakia, 25
France, 13, 24, 47
   Paris, 14
England, 12, 16, 25
   Birmingham, 27
   Blackpool, 53
   London, 46
     Chandos Street, 46
     Holborn, 1
     London Bridge, 17
     St. Paul's Cathedral, 46
   Yorkshire,
     Bolton Abbey, 3
     Craven, 3
     Harewood House, 65
   Windsor, 20
Germany, 45, 46, 48, 49
   Meissen, 45
Holland, 14, 15
   Amsterdam, 14, 15
     Coopers' and Winecrackers' Guild, 15
Hungary, 25, 43
India, 54, 55
Italy, 12, 59
   Piedmont, 48
   Sicily, 11
Portugal, Lisbon, 21
Scandinavia, 12, 49
Scotland, Aberdeenshire, Banchory 36
   Crathes Castle, 36
Spain, 13
Sweden, 49
   Uppsala, 49

Recipes using jiggers:
  Cocks' combs, artificial, 57
  Fried paste marvels, 58
  Muskedines called Rising Comfits or Vissing
     Comfits, *(sic)*, 62
  Muskedines called kissing comfites, 63
  Puits d'amour, 59

NOTES

Pastry Jiggers and Pastry Prints